The Little Yellow Book

Reclaiming the Liberal Democrats for the People

edited by Robert Brown and Nigel Lindsay

Liberal Futures

March 2012

An environmentally friendly book printed and bound in England by
www.printondemand-worldwide.com

Mixed Sources
Product group from well-managed
forests, and other controlled sources
www.fsc.org Cert no. TT-COC-002641
© 1996 Forest Stewardship Council
FSC

PEFC Certified
This product is
from sustainably
managed forests
and controlled
sources
PEFC
www.pefc.org
PEFC/16-33-415

This book is made entirely of chain-of-custody materials

www.fast-print.net/store.php

The Little Yellow Book
Copyright © Robert Brown and Nigel Lindsay 2012

ISBN 978-178035-266-4

First published 2012 by
FASTPRINT PUBLISHING
Peterborough, England.

Contents

About the Contributors

John Aldridge

John Aldridge was born in Dunfermline and brought up in Edinburgh. He joined the Young Liberals in 1967 and has been a member of the Scottish Liberal Party and later the Scottish Liberal Democrats since. After graduating from the University of Sussex, he was employed in several politics related jobs before joining the civil service. He worked for the Scottish Office and then Scottish Executive for about 30 years. His last post before retirement was Finance Director of the Scottish Executive.

Elspeth Attwooll

Elspeth Attwooll studied law, politics and philosophy at Queens College, Dundee before moving west to teach legal theory and comparative law at the University of Glasgow. Having joined the then Liberal Party at the age of 16, she was actively engaged with politics over the years, standing unavailingly for election at every government level. She finally made it into the European Parliament in 1999, serving until 2009, specialising in fisheries, employment & social affairs and regional policy.

After retirement Elspeth served for a while as convener of her local party but has now reverted to being a foot soldier. She remains engaged, however, with the European Movement in Scotland as well as being an Honorary Vice-President of both ALDTU and LYS and President of Liberal International (Scottish Branch) and the Scottish Women Liberal Democrats.

Robert Brown

Robert Brown obtained First Class Honours in Law at Aberdeen University in 1965. Qualifying as a solicitor, he served a period as Procurator Fiscal Depute in Dumbarton, before joining a large Glasgow legal firm where he became senior civil partner.

He was President of Aberdeen University Liberal Society and held various Party offices over the years, including around 10 years as Policy Convener of the Scottish Liberal Democrats, being responsible for a number of Party manifestos.

In 1977, Robert Brown was elected as the first Liberal Councillor in modern times in Glasgow, and remained undefeated until he stood down in 1992. He served as Liberal Democrat MSP for Glasgow from 1999 to 2011, and as Deputy Minister for Education from 2005 to 2007.

Ben Colburn

Dr Ben Colburn lectures in philosophy at Glasgow University. Prior to that he worked at the University of Cambridge, and was educated there and at Thomas Tallis

School in Greenwich. He writes on various topics in moral and political philosophy, including the foundations of liberalism, the nature of autonomy, authenticity and responsibility, and the philosophical bases of economic and educational policy.

Paul Coleshill

Paul Coleshill is Councillor for Langside Ward and the leader of the Liberal Democrats on Glasgow City Council. He has also served as Liberal Democrat Councillor for Rosneath ward in Argyll and Bute.

Paul holds several academic degrees and is a member of the Higher Education Academy as well as a Chartered Member of the CIPD. He was a lecturer in economics for over thirty years, latterly at the University of the West of Scotland.

He has studied and worked in Scotland for more than twenty years, and before that in England, Wales, Zambia, and Germany. He is partnered (civil) with a Democrat (liberal) from the US, whom he hopes to be allowed to marry.

Ross Finnie

Ross Finnie joined the Scottish Liberal Party in 1964. He has served on the national executive and was Chair of the Scottish Liberal Party from 1982 to 1986. He was a local councillor in Inverclyde for twenty two years from 1977 to 1999.

Ross was a Member of the Scottish Parliament from 1999 – 2011 and was the Cabinet Minister for Rural Affairs from 1999-2001 and for the Environment and

Rural Development 2001-2007. From 2007-2011 Ross was Shadow Secretary for Health and Wellbeing and depute convenor of the Health and Sport Committee. Ross is a Chartered Accountant by profession and worked for nearly thirty years in the financial services sector.

Gillian Gloyer

Gillian Gloyer is a long time Liberal activist. She held various executive positions in the Scottish Young Liberals throughout the 1980s, was chairperson from 1985-87 and International Vice-Chairperson from 1987-88.

Gillian now earns her living by fomenting democracy around the world. She has observed electoral processes throughout the Balkans and former Soviet Union (for the Organisation for Security and Cooperation in Europe) and in Latin America and the Arab world (for the European Union).

Gillian spent four years in Albania, running a long-term training programme with young political party activists. Elsewhere, she has run voter education programmes, trained national and international election observers and advised national election commissions. She lived in Chile during its transition from dictatorship to democracy and, through IFLRY (the International Federation of Liberal and Radical Youth), was active in East-West work in the mid-1980s.

Murray Leith

Murray Leith obtained his PhD from Glasgow University in 2006. He researches and lectures on

Scottish politics, national identity and nationalism, and US politics.

In 2009 he convened an international conference looking at the first decade of Scottish devolution, and in 2011 he published a book on nationalism and politics in Scotland.

Born in Scotland, Murray was raised in England and in his youth served in the Royal Navy, and travelled extensively as a result.

Nigel Lindsay

Nigel Lindsay studied Politics and International Relations at Aberdeen University where he was a leading figure in Young Liberal politics in Scotland. After postgraduate qualification, he became the first Liberal councillor in Aberdeen in 1973, serving until 1988 by which time the party had control of the city council. He then left party politics to become chief executive of a rural development agency in Lincolnshire, before moving back to Scotland at the time of devolution to take up a post in the Scottish Executive which he held until retirement.

Since returning to active politics in 2010, Nigel has worked with the European Movement in Scotland and the Scottish Liberal Democrats.

Denis Robertson Sullivan

Denis Robertson Sullivan was a founder member of the SDP and part of the negotiating team which achieved the merger with the then Liberal Party. He has severed the Liberal Democrats at almost every level, notably on the Federal and Scottish Executives. He has been UK Convenor of Finance and Administration and also Scottish Treasurer.

Denis is now trying to be retired, having just ended an 11 year direct association with Shelter, including a spell as UK Vice Chair and Scottish Chair. He is Chair of the Board of Scottish Hockey – a sport he did not play.

He has been a teacher, trade union official, director and managing director of his own businesses and has spent most of the last 10 years working directly or indirectly for charities and not for profit organisations.

Foreword

Willie Rennie MSP

Leader of the Scottish Liberal Democrats

The vigour of any political party can be measured by the level of debate that takes place within it on its principles and how these can be applied in action. A lively and constructive exchange of ideas shows the life and energy that runs through the party.

This book of essays demonstrates that Scottish Liberal Democrats are an intellectual force in the land, producing new ideas and stimulating debate on issues fundamental to the kind of Scotland we want to see. It proves that we choose to hold that debate in a context of mutual respect for each others' ideas. We eschew the all-out, bitter exchanges that so often characterise internal discussion within the Labour Party. Equally, we reject the supine acquiescence in the line from London that is the hallmark of Scottish Conservatives, or the similar way that the Leader's view is often accepted unquestioningly within the SNP.

Here is a book of ideas on how Liberalism can help build a better Scotland. The contributions it contains are by people who can think and who know what they are talking about. Some have held elected office in Scotland or Brussels, some have worked in government, and others are academics of high standing. All have worked over years for the Liberal Democrats because they believe our Party offers the best hope of building a Scotland which is fair, collaborative, and progressive.

The ideas debated within this book will not find everyone's agreement. Some of the authors see things differently from others within the spectrum of liberal opinion. Some of the ideas support current party policy, others suggest changes. My purpose in contributing this introduction is not to endorse all the ideas it contains, but to recommend it as thought-provoking, imaginative, and innovative. It shows our Party is thinking and working vigorously, and I welcome the debate it will bring.

Willie Rennie MSP

Preface

Liberalism in Scotland has had a remarkable record of success – the dominant political force in our country for a century until the 1920s, providing two out of six Liberal Prime Ministers (Rosebery and Campbell-Bannerman)[1] and nurturing no less than six Liberal or Liberal Democrat leaders since the war (Archie Sinclair, Jo Grimond, David Steel, Robert McLennan, Charles Kennedy and Menzies Campbell).

Scotland's traditional Burghs are still adorned by the municipal achievements and benevolence of local Liberals.

The New Liberalism that inspired the great Liberal Government of 1906 produced social and democratic reforms that marked the 20th century – progressive taxation, old age pensions and security against ill-health or unemployment, minimum wage legislation, continued

---

[1] Two more Liberal Prime Ministers – Gladstone and Asquith – sat for Scottish seats, as did Roy Jenkins as SDP Leader.

through the towering intellectual and political achievements of Beveridge and Keynes.

And the modern Liberal and Liberal Democrat revival since the 1960s has owed much to the campaigning success and personal qualities of the Scottish Party and its elected representatives. The Scottish Parliament itself is in many ways created in our image and by our thinking, while the success of Scottish Liberal Democrat Ministers from 1999-2007 in punching above their weight blazed a trail for Home Rule and democratic reform.

So the electoral cataclysm which befell the Party in the Scottish Parliament elections of May 2011 has caused much heart searching. There is a tendency to believe that the disaster was a tsunami from elsewhere and that normal service will soon be resumed; that the result was the joint product of the electoral unpopularity of Liberal Democrats in the United Kingdom Coalition Government and the successful capture of much of our political territory by an SNP Government which had caught and led the mood music of the time.

There is, no doubt, considerable truth in both these factors, but the contributors to this pamphlet believe, as do many others, that the seeds of the problem were planted long before, that the Scottish Liberal Democrats had lost our way since 2007, and had little by way of a persuasive message to offer to Scotland in 2011.

We also take the view that, while the scale of the financial crisis (as well as electoral arithmetic from the people) required a Coalition Government, this should be, in David Steel's words, strictly a business arrangement for agreed purposes and should not involve

Liberal Democrats signing up to a tone and direction of Government which is at odds with our beliefs and which goes down badly with our natural constituency.

We believe that the political challenges of the 21st century require a return to our Liberal Democrat roots and our core values, and a more rigorous debate about our political mission and message.

This pamphlet is deliberately named after the famous Liberal Yellow Book of 1928. The reason is that we are seeking to articulate a Liberalism of the people, that speaks to modern Scotland, that offers a radical and practical inspiration for the future that will offer hope to young people, a personal future and place to those damaged by the aftermath of the banking crisis, and a mission to make our country a more equal and buoyant one, not fractured by social division, hopelessness and inequality.

The Little Yellow Book is also intended to be something of a counterblast to the philosophy offered by the *Orange Book* of 2004. The *Orange Book* is well within the Liberal tradition and contains much of value to which Liberal Democrats can subscribe. But the belief that the private sector should be the driver of public services, that health services can be traded in a free market like widgets, that Government is a worse service-provider than monopoly private interests – these are not propositions we take to or regard as particularly Liberal.

On the contrary, we believe that a society where MPs, the media, the banks and the big institutions have all successively been found wanting points to the crying need for a more rigorous sense of public and personal ethics, and for a strengthened concept of the public interest – ideas which have been central to Liberalism since the days of Gladstone.

Scottish politics at present are particularly dispiriting. The Scottish Labour Party – once the home of people with a cause - is now weakened and largely a value-free zone. The dominant Nationalists have no vibrant and inclusive concept of Home Rule, no commitment to consensus in the constitutional apparatus of the State – but rather a belief in dividing people by national identity, in fracturing long-established personal links, and in reducing Scotland's place and standing in the world.

Scotland needs Liberal Democracy. These essays are a contribution to the vital debate on what our mission and message should be.

Chapter 1

Introduction

Robert Brown and Nigel Lindsay

An Unhappy Society

There is an odd paradox about 21st century society which should trouble us greatly.

On the one hand, the economic wealth of the world is many hundreds of times greater than a century ago – the technical ability to produce food, to provide material goods, to cater to demands not even conceived until recently.

Standards of housing, health, environment and social welfare, leisure opportunities, holidays are higher than ever before.

And yet, in Britain and much of the Western world, we are not happy. Many parts of our society are badly fractured, real opportunity and social mobility is less than it was 20 or 30 years ago, and many of our elites – politicians, bankers, top civil servants, the media, church leaders – have been shown to have feet of clay.

Levels of anxiety, stress and mental illness amongst both adults and young people are at record levels. More and more people seek refuge from their lives in drug addiction and alcohol. There are also many communities in the more deprived parts of our islands where life expectancy is at Third World levels and life chances are often blighted from and before birth.

The London riots of August 2011 were, to many people, a shock. Looting, arson, disorder, riot, which we associate with popular disturbances in less favoured nations, were to be seen nightly on our television screens in our own capital city. They did not seen to be specifically racial in character, nor to be confined to people in poverty. There was a strong impression of nihilism and unreason taking over. The motivations seemed to be boredom, greed, excitement, aggression or momentary madness. The disturbances vanished as quickly as they came. The irrational nature of the London riots was frightening, bewildering and disillusioning in equal measure.

The picture is not entirely bleak, of course. There are early signs of a willingness to challenge the conservative orthodoxy that has brought us to this pass, and to build a new and better society. Public fury at the excesses of executive pay is palpable and politicians have realised that more is required of them than spin and positioning. The "Occupy" movements in the UK, USA, and elsewhere may be naïve and unfocused, but they are at least a statement of dissatisfaction and may metamorphose into an influential voice. However, at the start of 2012 the challenges seem to outnumber the answers.

The Big Questions:

These challenges chime in with certain manifest failures of public policy and political discourse in our country:

- First, an identifiable loss of personal values and morality in a society which is more rootless than ever before. This can be described as a decline in Nonconformist values, and indeed we often forget how strongly such values have been embedded in our psyche over the last 500 years. These values include: notions of personal and family responsibility; considerate social behaviour; belief in the value of education; thrift and the importance of savings – but perhaps above all the ideas of progress and the improvement of society, of fair play and of duty to, and participation in, a wider society.

It is sometimes said that values of community in particular are more deeply entrenched in Scotland, but, in reality, the evidence suggests that social attitudes across the United Kingdom are remarkably homogenous.

- Second, the unbalanced and inequitable nature of income, wealth, opportunity and reward in our increasingly unequal society. This has two equally obnoxious extremes. At the top, there is the obscene grossness of top executive pay – where the link between effort and reward has been entirely abandoned and there is little connection to people's economic contribution and little sense of the broader public interest. At the bottom, there is the damaging and illiberal emergence of what is, we think, correctly identified as an underclass – people and communities who have no access to opportunity or even aspiration, whose lives are blighted as children by disasters of parental addiction, inadequacy and poverty, and a failure of motivation, multiplied by their presence in deprived communities.

There is a growing recognition of the fact that this is not just an issue of poverty in a financial sense, but of a wider social malaise, a loss of individual and community values.

- Third, the failure of the political parties even to articulate, far less to provide answers, to the key challenges in our society – and the helplessness of political leaders across Europe and America in the face of the financial whirlwind that followed the collapse of the traditional banking sector.

- Fourth, and linked to the preceding point, the timid nature of the mass media and its support for establishment values and viewpoints. Whether one looks at the large newspaper corporations whose owners are open about their support for wealth and privilege, or the BBC which relies on government support for licence fee rises, there is in UK media presentation of current affairs little to challenge the power elite. Investigative journalism is largely underground, and voices with something different to say are often excluded from the debate.

- Fifth, the growth and dominance of uncertainty, pessimism and fear. No one feels secure in their job or their income; if they are nearing retirement age, their pension level is under threat directly from low returns due to the collapse of the market and of interest rates, or indirectly as the Government faces up to the realities identified in the Hutton Report.

Young people are particularly disadvantaged – whether teachers or social workers, nurses or lawyers, or even worse school leavers, many simply cannot get jobs.

It is difficult to overestimate the damage that lack of job and life opportunities does to young people – the demoralisation of repeated failed job applications, the loss of power and control over lives, the demotivation and the sense that all effort and all skills are worthless.

The Liberal Democrat Approach:

The implications of these issues go into realms beyond traditional politics. They are hugely complex and difficult. The solutions are both national and international.

We don't have all the answers – we don't even yet have all the questions. But this is the territory Liberal Democrats should be in.

At their heart, they are about challenges which are meat and drink to Liberal Democrats – about arbitrary and excess power, about backing the public interest against sectional and selfish interests, about the lost hopes of a million young people killed off by the bankers and by their greed, about the failure of the political system to reflect and act on these issues, about the choices between right and wrong, and about freedom and opportunity too.

Liberalism, by its nature is a philosophy of optimism, and hope, of belief in young people, and of the progressive improvement of society. We believe in the value of education and of freedom and democracy for its own sake; we are against arbitrary or monopolistic power, privilege and corruption. We are on the side of localism, of community, and of the public interest. Perhaps above all we believe in the centrality of ordinary people over privilege, and the supremacy of politics over economics, and over economic theories in particular.

Putting the Market in its place

The contributors to this book all have their individual viewpoints and strongly held views, but share a philosophy of Liberalism which keeps the free market in its proper place – as a mechanism for organising the production, distribution and sale of goods, in itself amoral and apolitical, but very definitely the proper subject of political debate and regulation when it produces social ills – and a mechanism which has since 2008 gone very seriously wrong.

It is widely acknowledged that the ethos of Liberal Democrats in the Coalition owes much to a 2004 publication called *The Orange Book – reclaiming Liberalism*[2] with major contributions from Nick Clegg, Chris Huhne, David Laws, Vince Cable and others. Much of the Orange Book is good stuff, well within any definition

---

[2] ***The Orange Book: Reclaiming Liberalism*** edited by David Laws and Paul Marshall (Profile Books 2004). ISBN 1-86197-797-2)

of Liberalism, but some, particularly on public sector reform and the role of the private sector is, to our taste, more questionable.

Part of the motivation of the present book is to provide a critique of some of the *Orange Book* ideas, and part is to develop some of the ideas laid out in Robert Brown's June speech to the Social Liberal Forum (reproduced here) which owed a lot to conversations both of us had had with a number of people since the General Election, and more particularly since the Scottish elections.

Themes of this Book

The Free Market, disadvantage, responsibility and the general interest

Liberal academic **Ben Colburn** takes the lead by making the case for alternative approaches equally, if not more Liberal than that contained in the Orange Book. No doubt every age has its own tone, but Ben makes the important point that there is nothing inevitable about the current political and policy direction of our country. Indeed Nick Clegg and other Liberal Democrats in Government have been increasingly talking about issues like increasing social mobility, tackling excess pay and inequalities and looking again at employee participation in companies.

In sketching out alternatives, Ben puts the "free" market in context – "neither poison nor panacea", its importance varying according to context, favoured where, as often, it means a wider range of options, but much more complex when advocated in areas of public services and public "goods".

He warns of the dangers of monopoly and oligarchy, and of lack of effective information and choice which can end up by degrading not enhancing public services.

Ben goes on to develop the idea of personal autonomy as a key component of the Liberal approach, but to remind us also – in the wake of the irresponsible greed of the bankers – that there is an important role for personal and corporate responsibility, ethics and the general interest. Responsibility, he argues, is "precluded by the dominance of powerful commercial interests" which are, if anything, more of a threat to liberty and free choice than state power. Accordingly privatising particular public services is not the answer if it doesn't increase individual responsibility.

Further, freedom and responsibility both require the removal of disadvantage – poverty, lack of opportunity, and all the rest. Indeed he argues the case for strong public services, communally funded and delivered, precisely on Liberal grounds – that they enhance individual freedom of all of us, and discharge some of our communal duties to each other. Ben concludes his essay with some thoughts on the renewal of our decaying democracy, the value of the Liberal Democrat community politics approach and for reconnecting political thinking with the real world, rather than the world of focus-group junkies.

Multiple Identities and the need for a Written Constitution

Murray Leith is also an academic who has done a lot of thinking about personal and national identity. He applies his analysis to the debate on the future constitutional settlement of Scotland and the United Kingdom. Like the Scottish Liberal Democrats' *Steel Commission on Moving to Federalism*, Murray argues that most people in Scotland identify quite happily with multiple identities – Scottish, British, European, regional, religious, professional, personal.

Murray articulates clearly the lack of developed constitutional thinking in the United Kingdom about the implications of Devolution or indeed Federal Home Rule. He echoes the call from UK Federal Deputy Leader Simon Hughes MP for an English Parliament and examines the implications of this for the constitutional argument.

Murray's essay and the sophisticated work done by Liberal Democrats through the Steel Commission, the Calman Commission, the current Scotland Bill and now the Campbell Commission point to the need for a federal end point to the constitutional argument, but also how far England has to go to catch up with constitutional developments around her.

The Cost of the Market and Public Services

John Aldridge and Paul Coleshill both take further the issue of the place of the market in public services. The one a high flying civil servant, recently retired; the other an academic and local Councillor with both practical and theoretical knowledge of the place of the market – John and Paul mount a powerful defence of the public interest, rather than economic doctrine or managerial jargon, as the key determinant in how we run our public services.

The dichotomy between the alleged beneficial role of the private sector and the "millstone" theory of the public sector is false, but equally, as John argues, there is a need for economy, efficiency and effectiveness in the public sector. He points out the inevitable tendency towards monopoly in the private sector, and argues that, if a service is already a monopoly, it is easier and cheaper to regulate it in the public sector – a lesson which could have usefully been learnt before rail privatisation. The litmus test should be effectiveness.

The downsides of cutting costs, the lack of spare capacity in an absolutely efficient service, the neglect of quality and effectiveness – these are the challenges in our public services, particularly in a time of relative austerity. John makes a strong case for preferring local and flexible services rather than centralised ones, and for a sensible approach which does not over-regulate and constrain third sector organisations who are often good at providing innovation and flexibility. He points out too the limits of structural reorganisation – that you still need roughly the same number of people to do the job.

Paul Coleshill identifies correctly the very high cost (to the public purse) of maintaining markets, particularly in contract construction monitoring and enforcement. He attacks the proliferation of ALEOS and other arms-length bodies which – largely for tax and technical reasons - have removed democratic control from many Council services in Glasgow (and elsewhere), and argues for a restoration of democracy in local government. His argument that no one understands the new structures is valid too – why has it been necessary to disguise the Parks, Roads, Housing and Cleansing Departments under such linguistic contortions as "Department of Enterprise Resources" or even "Department of Democratic Accountability"? George Orwell would be proud!

A more equal and less corrupt society

Nigel Lindsay notes the shallow concept of "freedom to dine at the Ritz" in arguing for greater equality of opportunity and power in our country. He draws on international experience, not least in Scandinavia, to show that more equal societies, and ones too where local government organisation is community-based, are far better placed to deliver effective public services and contribute to a happier, healthier and less fractured society.

In particular, Nigel demolishes the myth, beloved of centralising SNP Ministers, that Scotland has too many local government organisations, pointing out that smaller, more local organisations on the Continent get more public "buy in". He also notes that the Scandinavian countries are amongst the least corrupt in the worlds – a position once held by the UK before its modern outsourcing of chunks of the civil service.

Finally, Nigel reaffirms the high priority that Liberal Democrats should attach to funding effective public services and attacks the idea that the country can no longer afford these – in stark contrast to our ability to fund a variety of hugely expensive military adventures abroad. Nigel draws evidence on the issue of inequality from the influential book *The Spirit Level* which showed how damaging to society is the unbalanced and inequitable nature of income, wealth and opportunity in Britain, and from the OECD Life Satisfaction Index – and attempt to measure scientifically a subjective matter which should be at the heart of Liberal concerns..

Obscenities of power and wealth

This is a theme developed by **Robert Brown** who also draws on the work of the *High Pay Commission* to attack what he rightly calls the "obscenities of power and wealth". Robert notes too the strong case for regarding excessively high remuneration – particularly if unlinked to performance – as being a significant causal factor in the financial collapse of 2008. The corollary – and consequence – of excessively high pay – is the unacceptable phenomenon of an underclass where people's lives and opportunities are blighted before birth.

Robert identifies the fear and uncertainty which now corrodes the sense of wellbeing of many people in our society – and not least the damaging demoralisation of young people unable to get a job. These, he says, are very much Liberal issues, arising from arbitrary and excess power, loss of opportunity and the failure of the political system and its elites, combined with a lack of accountability of bloated and overlarge organisations.

He calls for a range of measures to end the bonus culture and the closed cabal which decides top pay, to tackle the distorting effects of excessive high pay, to reform company law to make companies more responsive to their employees and to the public interest, and to look at the idea of a Robin Hood Tax, first mooted by Keynes, to recoup for the public benefit some offset to the damage done to ordinary people by financial services greed.

Instant gratification and Political Leadership

Former MEP **Elspeth Attwooll** draws out the connections between the national UK financial deficit and the debt levels of individual households. Much of this goes back to the modern consumer society and the ethos of instant gratification which is so stimulated by the pressures of commercial advertising.

She points out how political decisions are too often controlled or led by financial markets or by the media, that a short-term panic – and reactive - approach is more or less built into major decisions which have substantial impacts on our lives.

Elspeth calls attention to the importance of robust – and liberal – political leadership, based not on the cult of personality, but firmly grounded in the political principles and tradition of our Party. She notes a discord between the "Orange Bookery" of the Party leadership and the lack of conviction by many grassroots members, particularly in Scotland, that an over-reliance on economic liberalism is the way forward.

Power to the People

Denis Robertson Sullivan brings his vast experience of public and not-for-profit organisations to bear in mapping out ideas on how to give body to concepts of localism and local empowerment. For many of us, local and community empowerment could be the dynamo of a fresh influx of strength to our democracy.

Denis has the simple but powerful view that the more individuals invest in their communities, then the more they will value it and benefit from it. The more individuals participate in our society at every level and especially locally, then the stronger our democracy will be. It is the leitmotif of our longstanding support for community politics as both a style and a philosophy of political campaigning - and it gives strength and vigour to our Party's cause when opinion poll ratings are at the famous asterisk level!

In many ways, local institutions and loyalties are still hugely powerful – the identity of the old Burghs and Royal Burghs, the strength of community institutions, clubs and voluntary groups. The institutions of Government must recognise and use these building blocks – indeed we know municipalities and communes are the bulwark of successful democracy in many parts of Europe.

But what about a more democratic and liberal view of land itself? Common good is an ancient concept much in need of adaptation to modern needs. Surely the community should have rights, particularly in lad or buildings unused or abandoned by private owners or public bodies?

Denis argues too that there could be greater use made of existing community assets and sources of wealth – community windfarms producing energy and revenue for local communities, the use of housing association assets to underwrite further investment in the community, the idea of a Government "golden share".

What are the key public goods?

Ross Finnie brings his formidable intellectual powers to bear on looking at the inter-relation between the big personal expenditures required by our people – tertiary education, house purchase, provision for old age, and personal care. He argues that education at tertiary level is an investment by society for the benefit of society and that the case for tuition fees, upfront or as a graduate levy of some sort, is ill-conceived – the cost is better and indeed more efficiently met from progressive taxation.

Indeed, even the new English arrangements introduced by the Coalition Government, and for which Liberal Democrats unnecessarily sacrificed so much of their credibility, will increase public expenditure through this parliament and into the next. Even beyond that, no forecaster suggests a significant reduction in cost.

However Ross identifies that there are other issues to be considered in this debate – the stubbornly low levels of young people from poorer backgrounds going to University, and issues of choice and Government limits on the type of degree available.

Housing, unlike education, is not a classic public good but most Liberal Democrats regard a decent home and environment as a high priority in a Liberal society. However Ross is rightly concerned about the contribution unsustainable house prices had to make to the financial collapse, and argues strongly against the idea that recovery means a return to business as before. Instead he renews the relevance of the traditional Liberal advocacy of Land Value tax as a replacement for Council tax and business rates.

Finally Ross considers the challenge of funding for old age, the mistake probably made by Beveridge in opting for a pay as you go approach to this, and the need to arrive at a more sustainable longer term solution, possibly based in time on a fully funded national insurance scheme. The work of Steve Webb as Pensions Minister in committing the Government to a major uprating of future pensions and a record rise in current state pensions is a major – and rather unheralded success for Liberal Democrats in the Coalition Government.

Major challenge to re-engage with people

In the final chapter, **Gillian Gloyer** uses her long experience as a United Nations and EU monitor and democracy adviser, and her first hand experience of the aftermath of the break up of the Communist hegemony in Eastern Europe, and now of the Arab Spring revolutions in Egypt and Tunisia, to consider the lessons that British democracy could learn from these new, young, sometimes struggling but immensely hopeful eruptions in the Middle East.

She notes that, despite long established Opposition political parties in many Arab countries, the revolutions were often led by young people and by women – a notable feature in an otherwise very conservative region. Elections were in the event the way in which the old political elites re-established themselves, not a very happy conclusion.

There are manifold lessons for Scottish Liberal Democrats – the low level of political discourse here, a media with little diversity of view, alienation between Government and people. Gillian's conclusion is that there is a major challenge for us to find language which people understand and to communicate it so that it reaches the people. It echoes the cry for a more principled and inspiring leadership which we noted from Elspeth Attwooll earlier.

Summary

We make no pretence of covering every area. The essays have touched on but not developed many important issues of poverty and deprivation, of sustainability and the environment, of the role of education and whether our schools are as good as they could be, of the major priority of young people in the care system, of the causes of criminal offending and how to reduce it. These issues are hugely important and merit separate treatment – some of which we may return to in the future. However, we hope this book will stimulate debate, provide a litmus test for Liberal Democrats on the Coalition's programme, and lead to a rebirth and renewal of Liberal ideas.

Above all, we want to see an end of the politics based on focus groups, of "positioning", and of telling people what it is thought they want to hear.

As Henry Ford once said:

"If I'd asked people what they wanted when I started out, they'd have said 'A faster horse'."[3]

The role of leadership in politics is much neglected. A decent leader with the right language and approach could kill all the focus group industry dead in its tracks.

---

[3] Quoted in the obituary of Steve Jobs of Apple Computers

Liberalism is a questioning, radical cause which needs to have a programme which appeals to our hearts, which inspires us with its worth and its value and which differentiates us from others.

Chapter 2

The Setting – *Liberal Democracy in Scotland: the Way Forward*

Robert Brown

An edited version of a speech given to the Social Liberal Forum in Glasgow 25th June 2011

There is nothing like a major defeat to make individuals and parties reassess themselves – but it is not an occurrence to be welcomed nevertheless!

In order to look forward, we first have to look back, to identify what went wrong and be realistic about the causes, to ask what sort of people Liberal Democrats are and what we believe, to examine the challenges, and to begin to plot the way forward.

I have always believed that Liberalism and Liberal Democracy has been over the years a more coherent, principled and radical political philosophy by far than anything else on offer in British or Scottish politics. It is a source of inspiration and reinvigoration in difficult times, a litmus test of what is right for our country and a solid foundation for hope and optimism in our future.

Now, to say the least, these are difficult times. The disaster of 5th May cannot be understated – we hold no constituency seats in mainland Scotland, our constituency share across Scotland was 7.93% of the vote – the regional list vote 5.2% and only 2.5% in Glasgow. It was the worst result in Scotland since 1950.

It is true, of course, that a major cause of the Liberal Democrat collapse was the view taken by the voters of the Coalition Government. I support the Coalition but I take David Steel's view on it, that "the coalition is a business arrangement born of necessity to clear up the country's dire financial debt. It should never be portrayed as anything else."

But we have paid a huge price for the failures of our leaders to realise that trust was our strongest asset, that you can't retain trust by selling out on our most identifiable policy, on which our MPs had made personal pledges, that back slapping on the front bench between Nick Clegg and Danny Alexander and the Tory leadership was the crassest of political blunders, and that a Coalition Agreement which works must require sign up in advance to major new policies. Suggestions that Liberal Democrat leaders agreed to sell out on tuition fees well in advance of the election because they themselves opposed the policy simply add to the image of untrustworthiness.

Nevertheless there is no mileage, in my view, in attempting to pretend the Coalition is nothing to do with

Scottish Liberal Democrats, because it defines, for better or worse, our strongest public image.

And I believe it would be a huge mistake to believe that our defeat was nothing to do with the Scottish campaign or the Scottish Liberal Democrats.

The truth is actually stark and depressing and one we need to recognise. There was no substantial reason to vote Liberal Democrat at the Scottish elections. All the glossy, unread newspapers in the world, the blue letters, the targeting are no use if the central strategy and messages are not up to the job.

There was no message to set the heart racing – indeed it was difficult to discern a message at all. There was no narrative as to our view of Scotland going forward. There were no big ideas, and no obvious strategy. There was no strong connection between manifesto ideas and the core values of the Party. There was nothing for urban voters.

Above all, there was the trust issue – the evil fairy begotten of the tuition fees debacle in England – which infected our supporters, destroyed our confidence and killed our vote.

So where do we go from here?

Our central challenge is to rediscover our own tone and language, to rebuild that trust and to widen the constituency to which we can appeal – and to offer a more attractive appeal as a national Party than the SNP.

The first thing is for us to understand and have confidence in our political beliefs and values. This meeting today is held under the banner of the Social

Liberal Forum – but can I challenge the very title of Social Liberal? Social Liberalism is Liberalism; it is Liberal Democracy. We should not allow our Party and our philosophy to be stolen from us by the New Right, by the neo-liberals, by those who believe that freedom means primarily economic freedom - the unrestricted freedom of the market, rather than the freedom of people or communities. Markets, for us, have never been "tools of unrestricted wealth accumulation divorced from any concept of the public interest"

Let me quote from an article by Simon Kovar in the Liberal magazine last year which may help us to focus on the key themes and drivers of our cause. Simon Kovar said this:

> *Successive generations of Liberal Democrat leaders and politicians, whether of the party's left or right, have held the following in common. They have fought privilege and corruption; they have argued for a redistribution of wealth and opportunity from the rich to the poor; they have regarded the market as a (limited) means and not an (un-checked) end; and they have recognised the moral limits of markets. They have argued in support of public services and, when they have spoken of public service reform, they have meant alternative means of **public** provision, not privatisation.* [4]

The late Conrad Russell believed that Liberalism as a philosophy is primarily concerned with the use and dispersal of power. "Beveridge," he said, "trying to protect people from the giants of poverty and want, came

---

[4] Simon Kovar – The Neo Liberal Democrats – The Liberal magazine Aug 2010

from the same tradition as (John) Locke trying to protect them against an arbitrary king. It is a tradition of protecting individuals from the effects of arbitrary power."

Now surely the last few years have seen arbitrary power at its most obscene.

- The Iraq War, built on American and British power, without international sanction;

- The power of huge supermarket companies to undermine local economies, impose themselves on local communities, dictate terms to local Councils and local suppliers, and distort food supply chains.

- Above all, the greed and recklessness of the banks which brought down the world economy, destroyed the life chances of individuals and the prosperity of nations, and handed unimaginably huge dollops of money to its top executives – banks which were too big for Governments to allow them to fail.

I am in no sense a Socialist leveller down – but I must say I find the pay package of £7.5 million paid to the Royal Bank Chief Executive obscene, regardless of the justification that it is the going rate. I also find the creep in the salaries of top executives in the service of Government, Quangos, Councils and Universities to anything up to the £1/4 million mark, often together with bonuses, to be distinctly questionable. These are matters on which Liberal Democrats should have a view because they destroy any sense of fairness and common purpose in our country.

I am a "condition of the people" Liberal Democrat – I think most of us here are. For me, equality of opportunity; enhancing the life chances of young people; balancing the disadvantage which afflicts so many, not least in Glasgow, from and before their birth; the liberating power of education; the quality of communities and the urban environment. These things are the essence of Liberal democracy, the fulfilment of our defence of the rights of the individual.

And along with the ideas I have mentioned – fighting arbitrary power, breaking down monopoly, fighting privilege and corruption, good quality public services, we can add the theory of ascending power - that power comes from and is conferred by the people – and the concept of pluralism which means the dispersal of power and the promotion of diversity. The idea of localism which is a powerful, if ill-developed, idea in our lexicon, is linked to these themes. So is our support for the Voluntary sector - and our view of a federal future for Scotland and the United Kingdom.

And one might add that Liberalism also backs a vigorous view of the public interest – from Gladstone counting every paper clip in the Treasury, to Vince Cable warning about the debt mountain and the unsustainable prices in the housing market, from open competition in the civil service in the 1860s to opposition to a single Scottish police force in 2011. Contrast that with New Labour, a party at ease with the excesses of the filthy rich, or the SNP who take money equally readily and without scruple from Edwin Morgan, the late Scots Makar and a gay man, and from Sir Brian Soutar, the backer of Section 28; from Sir Sean Connery, who offers support to the SNP from the comfort and ambiguity of tax exile – or for that matter a party which lavishes SNP Ministerial access and bias on Donald Trump.

I have talked about values. Values should lead to our narrative – about renewing the United Kingdom and Scotland's place in it, refocusing our identity in a post nationalist age. Home Rule means more powers for a purpose for the Scottish Parliament within a reformed United Kingdom.

We must develop and give meaning to the idea of localism. This is not, as many of our Councillors believe, just a matter of central Government surrendering power to Councils. Councils, Liberal Democrat led or otherwise, should set the local strategy but don't always have that great a record of truly empowering local communities, social enterprises and the voluntary sector. And there must be solid, clear and attractive ideas that speak the language of the voter.

And a narrative too about young people. If young people support us in greater numbers, there is inevitable growth over the years. If nationalism is old fashioned – as I believe it is; if Labour has lost its soul and purpose – as it has - a principled non-ideological but values-driven Liberal Democrat Party is well-placed; If people are rejecting traditional politics, a community based campaigning Party has the ball at its feet; If the electorate is becoming more middle class and aspirational, if it travels more, it is more in our image.

We need – and we have lost - optimism, hope and a sense of progress. We must be the Party of the future, uniting demographic, political and social trends.

Above all, the narrative should help the debate be fought on our territory, not someone else's.

What about the way forward inside the Party? We need to reignite debate and discussion and passion about our cause, to write pamphlets and articles, to encourage new thinking, to engage with academics and others with ideas. We need to identify and take forward those ideas on the basis of our values and our narrative, hone them with the voters, challenge our Party at Conference, fight over them in local supper clubs, imbue our elected representatives and candidates with them and train our people, not least our young people, in the language and values of Liberal Democracy.

And, if the direction of these ideas is not that of the Coalition or the leadership, or the Orange Book, we need to have the analytical tools to engage in and win the arguments, to understand and debate the issues around public sector "reform" in particular, the role of the private sector and what we want for schools, and hospitals and the NHS. Because the Party is our Party, held in trust by the present leadership for the future, built on the traditions of the past.

I know there will be some people here today who take the view that the leadership are closet-Tories, that they have sold out the Party's soul for Ministerial office, that the new leadership project is to reposition us on the centre right. I don't share that view, but there are undoubtedly areas where the actions of the Coalition and of our Ministers seem at odds with the instincts of the Party. Coalition is a tricky place to be and a strong and assertive Party can strengthen the extent to which Liberal things – things which affect the worse off in society - happen in our Government. Liberal Democrats are not, as indeed Nick Clegg said in a major speech last July, in favour of reducing the size of the state as a matter of ideology, but equally we shouldn't take hard earned cash from ordinary people to spend on bureaucracy, waste or inefficiency.

I confess I am uncertain how best to widen the ground on which we stand, which currently looks a bit like one of these English coastal villages where the sea has eroded the coastline and demolished everything within 100 yards of the previous beach. It is part confidence and credibility, part relevance of message, part the excitement of new ideas and modern mood music, part identifying and playing to our "constituencies" of interest – which would previously have been the progressive middle classes, the young and aspiring, women, and rural Scotland but had increasingly become a section of the urban electorate.

Our challenge has become immeasurably tougher following our defeat in May. We have, in my view, the right man to lead us in Willie Rennie – the one positive outcome of the elections, but a crucial one. Willie is already articulating our values; he is a man used to winning, and he has the combination of the common touch and personal authority which is needed for the battles ahead. Our cause will be immeasurably helped if he and we can ignite an intellectual ferment within and beyond the Party.

Our belief as Liberal Democrats was eloquently expressed in the pamphlet "We can conquer unemployment (1928):

> *We believe with a passionate faith that the end of all political and economic action is not the perfecting or perpetuation of this or that piece of machinery or organisation, but that individual men and women may have life and that they may have it more abundantly.*

But let me finish with a quote, as one must in difficult times, from Russell Johnston on the importance of Liberalism. Not the one about climbing the mountain and seeing the peak, because we have fallen off that mountain, but one from the 1984 Conference in Ayr.[5]

> *Freedom,* he said, *simply for the self to do as he or she wants, if it is not joined with a responsibility to care for the freedom of others, is no more than the pursuit of privilege, the badge of Conservatism through the ages. There is no freedom for the poor.*
>
> *...Liberalism has within it the dream that the good and the courageous spirit that resides within mankind can be given release.*
>
> *It is for these things that we walk the wet streets; it is for these things that we commit our time and treasure; and it is these things that we will one day bring to pass.*

---

[5] Just Russell – The collected speeches of Sir Russell Johnston MP 1979-1986 p56 – published by the Scottish Liberal Party

I make no apology for ending on this note, with recollection of days when Liberals were confident in their beliefs, because our cause – the cause of Liberal Democracy – remains a great cause, needed in Scotland and beyond, and is something to be confident and optimistic about.

Chapter 3

Liberalism for the people – *The Orange Book* challenged

Ben Colburn

This essay is an attempt to prompt more direct and
public argument about political theory in the Liberal
Democrats. Such argument is the best way to address two
dangerous illusions that we face: the lazy attraction of
woolly thinking, and a sense of inevitability about the
political direction in which we are travelling. These
illusions are damaging both to our party and to politics in
general: they serve only to stultify our collective
imagination, and to lend unwitting assistance to an
unsatisfactory status quo. Plainly, the Liberal Democrats
should have no truck with these things. We have always
been prepared to question conventional wisdom, seeking
radical alternatives even when these rock the boat or
prove unpopular and uncomfortable. More than most,
we can justly claim to have no truck with the covert
motives that in other places might welcome lack of
rigour and scrutiny.

To that end, in what follows I set out a challenge to the only serious recent attempt to set out an intellectual manifesto for Liberalism, namely *The Orange Book* edited by Paul Marshall and David Laws. I offer some friendly criticisms of the theses in that book, and demonstrate that it doesn't set out the only intellectually rigorous option for understanding Liberalism. In the process I propose an alternative set of principles which might form the basis of a different intellectual and political direction for us to take.

This might sound like an invitation to navel-gazing: getting our house in theoretical order is all very well, but might seem a distraction from the practical business of politics. I will conclude by suggesting that the very opposite is true. If we are to rejuvenate British politics, then more robust Liberal engagement with political ideas is vital: it should be at the heart of the community politics which we rightly regard as our greatest strength.

Part 1: Opening up the intellectual terrain

There might seem to be something contradictory about what I've just said. On the one hand, I'm complaining about the lack of rigorous thinking in the Liberal Democrats, and its bad effects on policy and political practice. On the other, I have just acknowledged the presence of *The Orange Book*, which exemplifies precisely the hard-headed rigour for which I'm calling.

The problem is precisely that *The Orange Book* is so very singular. Being alone in the landscape, it dominates effortlessly, and the principles that it contain acquire a stature which they perhaps would not if it weren't so isolated. By dint of being the only serious and rigorous intellectual manifesto for the party produced in recent years, it becomes the default option for someone dissatisfied with the sort of woolly thinking I decry above.

This is a bad state of affairs. The intellectual achievement of *The Orange Book* is done scant justice if nobody within the party engages with it on the same terms. Serious thinking deserves serious scrutiny. Moreover, it does little good for the Liberal Democrats if we labour under the impression that the market-oriented Liberalism set out there is the only option. We are in enough danger of sabotaging ourselves with illusions of inevitability in other areas, as Robert Brown observes elsewhere in this volume. We must avoid allowing such illusions to stultify our collective theoretical imagination too.

My argument for an alternative begins with David Laws's essay 'Reclaiming Liberalism'. Laws complains there about what he calls '*a la carte* Liberalism': that is, a political position not motivated by sound and consistent Liberal principles, but rather composed of a mish-mash of apparently worthy causes, adopted piecemeal with no overall theoretical framework.

Laws is right that we should avoid this. The danger of such an approach is that, while each of these policies might seem well-intentioned in context, it leads a fractured and contradictory picture overall. The chance of a clear and distinctive Liberal voice is lost, and we rightly stand accused of saying different things in different places because it suits us. No doubt there's nothing mendacious about the tension. The local councillor who advocates more road furniture as a way of combating speeding, and the MP who decries interference in individual liberties, are no doubt both sincere; and it's quite possible that rigorous Liberal principles might show how these apparently conflicting commitments can be reconciled. The problem is that the failure to articulate clear general principles underlying our policies gives the *impression* of their being an opportunistic pick and mix, even when they're not.

It is ironic, then, that Laws's position itself looks like an instance of the *a la carte* Liberalism which he decries. Here's why. Laws identifies four central commitments of the Liberal tradition: personal liberty, political liberty, economic liberty, and social liberty. The first consists in freedom from interference and coercion; the second in participation in the political system; the third in private property rights and the ability to participate in a free market; and the fourth in possessing the necessary internal and external resources to use the other types of freedom for individual and societal betterment. The balanced combination of these elements is, in his view, what Liberalism really consists in, and the need to return to it is what motivates the central proposal of 'Reclaiming Liberalism', namely the restoration of economic liberty to centre stage in Liberal Democrat thinking.

This ignores the fact that the four strands Laws identifies are themselves unhappy bedfellows. True, they have all been elements of the Liberal heritage, albeit in different combinations and with different emphasis at different times. That history, however, doesn't mean that all four elements can unproblematically now be combined. To take one example, unconstrained economic liberty tends over time to lead to large inequalities in wealth and influence. Such inequalities impede political liberty because of their negative impact on people's ability to participate in the political system on an even footing. To take another example, trying to promote social liberty sometimes leads to people having less personal liberty than they might otherwise have. Laws himself quotes a speech by Joseph Chamberlain in 1885, in which the latter evokes exactly this sort of tension:

> *The great problem of our civilization is still unresolved. We have to account for, and to grapple with, the mass of misery and destitution in our midst, co-existent as it is with the evidence of abundant wealth and teeming prosperity. It is a problem which some men would set aside with references to the eternal laws of supply and demand, to the necessity of freedom of contract, and to the sanctity of every private right of property. But gentlemen, these phrases are the convenient cant of selfish wealth.*

In other words, in our current unjust world, we can't pursue all four types of liberty at the same time: there are some elements of economic and personal liberty that clash with social and political liberty, in the sense that an overzealous protection of the former prevents us from properly realising the latter. Let's leave aside (for now) Chamberlain's view that social and political liberty are the more important priorities. The point here is just that we can't always have all the freedoms we might want, because in a non-ideal world the different types of liberty aren't always mutually supportive. So, the assumption that they can be harmoniously combined and pursued in tandem is unrealistic, and also dangerous, because it conceals the costs of giving one of the four strands greater emphasis. All of which is to say: if (as we should) we take seriously Laws's injunctions against *a la carte* Liberalism, we should worry that his own positive proposals are guilty of precisely the sins he decries.

Of course, we could recast Laws's essay somewhat, so that instead of trying unrealistically to combine all elements of our Liberal heritage, it instead simply proposes a version of Liberalism with economy liberty given priority. That would avoid the unwarrantedly optimistic assumption that it will never run into conflict with the protection of other forms of liberty; and it would allow us to appreciate the essay for what it is, namely a clear and articulate case for one particular way of understanding what Liberalism is based on, and what policies it should inform.

Nevertheless, it should now be clear that Laws's Liberalism is only one possible theoretical position we might take. We should not let its rigour deceive us into thinking it is the only option. After all, there is an opposite sin to the lazy pick-and-mix approach behind *a la carte* Liberalism, which is to assume (equally lazily), once we've found one rigorous and well-motivated version of Liberalism, that is the only option on the table. No doubt none of the contributors to *The Orange Book* actually think this. The *Book* is an attempt to provoke healthy debate rather than to silence it. But reading the essays unwarily, it is easy to get the impression that the only way to avoid *a la carte* Liberalism is to accept this economic-liberty-focussed proposal in its entirety.

That impression is false, for two reasons. First, once it's understood that attempting to combine all four historic elements of Liberalism is as *a la carte* as anything else, we might choose instead to emphasise personal, or political, or social Liberalism: there's no reason to think in advance that such a theory couldn't be as rigorous and consistent as the focus on economic liberty that Laws advocates. Second, it's not as though *The Orange Book* itself lacks internal diversity. Different chapters offer detailed proposals in particular areas, and offer different visions of what Liberalism is. The vision for environmental policy set out by Susan Kramer in her chapter (to take one especially persuasive example) differs in its principles from the proposals for deregulation and tax policy offered by Vince Cable in his; both sets of proposals differ from Laws's ideas as set out in his chapters on the nature of Liberalism and on health policy. The media has attempted to portray *The Orange Book* as a homogenous manifesto by a group of doctrinaire crypto-conservatives. In fact, of course, it displays all the subtlety and diversity that is the hallmark of true Liberal politics.

Part 2: Sketching an Alternative

So far, I've argued that it would be a mistake to read *The Orange Book* thinking that it offers the only credible theory of Liberalism that we might accept. The *Book* itself contains scope for various different acceptable ways of construing Liberalism, and there's no reason to think that it has a monopoly on rigour. I now turn to my second task, which is to offer a friendly contribution to the debate which I think deserves hearing and elaboration alongside the *Orange Book* proposals, concentrating on the attitude we should have to economic liberty and market mechanisms, especially in the delivery of public services.

My starting point here is an argument, alluded to especially by Laws and Ed Davey, in favour of localism. The gist is this: politics is imperfect, nobody is omniscient, and for complex problems there are no simple solutions. The best we can do, in light of this, is to seek answers by harnessing our collective political creativity and being sensitive to contextual variation. This is a central Liberal insight. It informs our enthusiasm for experimentation, and it vindicates our willingness to embrace the complexities arising in variation, diversity and difference.

It is a mistake to think, as some do, that this line of thought tells unequivocally in favour of the free market. The market is no more a panacea than any other proposal. Context is all. A proper Liberal approach to the use of market mechanisms in public life will recognize this, by recognizing *both* the power of those mechanisms for promoting the common good, and *also* the different constraints necessary, in different circumstances, for that pursuit to be fair and successful. In some contexts, a perfectly free market will be appropriate. In others, a constrained market is better. In yet others, we may need to avoid market forces entirely, precisely because certain sorts of public service being beyond their purview is a necessary precondition of the market being fair and successful in other domains.

It might look as though this is exactly the sort of *a la carte* Liberalism Laws warns against, but it is not. We must have a well-motivated and harmonious set of core principles, and must be consistently and rigorously true to those principles. But, as I've said, Liberals also recognize (in a way that proponents of other political creeds sometimes don't) that the same principles may imply different actions in different circumstances. That might *look* like an incoherent pick and mix, but it's not. It's the result of recognizing one of the deep truths of Liberal politics, namely the importance of sensitivity to context.

In the present discussion, this means that Liberals should reject the simple dichotomies offered to us by other political ideologies. The free market is neither poison nor panacea, because there is no such thing as *the* free market. Civil society is a complex and messy mosaic of subtly different arrangements in different domains of public life, varying in design and intent according to context. Against this background, the apparent unity of 'the market' is just another one of the procrustean illusions to which the proponents of non-Liberal political theories are so prone.

The properly Liberal approach eschews both extremes, and is thus neither wholly pro- nor anti-market. Instead, it takes each domain as it comes, and asks: is it appropriate for a market mechanism to function here? Can we expect it to work well? What sort of market mechanism? What background do we need to have in place for it to work well? As Vince Cable says in his contribution to *The Orange Book*, 'the issue ... is rarely one of absolute ideological clarity, but of where the shifting boundaries are and should be.'

Deciding where those boundaries lie means considering the general principled constraints that we should bring to a case-by-case examination. Cable suggests the following: protecting and promoting individual freedom of choice; avoiding monopoly providers; decentralization; preventing problems rather than curing them; limiting the overall size of the public sector; and seeking efficiency and value for money. Of these, the first plays the most role important in Cable's argument. The promotion of individual choice is motivated by the powerful ideals of personal and social liberty, and it is also what underwrites the other conditions listed (so, for example, the problem with a purely reactive rather than preventative attitude to public health is that it promotes a culture of dependency which undermines individual freedom).

In what follows, I extend Cable's set of principles. I agree that the protection of individual choice should be one of our guiding lights, though I suggest that Cable hasn't quite worked out in full what this concern requires. I also argue that we must supplement this with a principle of respect for individual responsibility.

We should protect and promote individual choice, because people's lives go better if they enjoy personal and social liberty. For one thing, it allows individuals to decide for themselves what lives they want to lead. As John Stuart Mill said,

> *Human nature is not a machine to be built after a model, and set to do exactly the work prescribed for it, but a tree, which requires to grow and develop itself on all sides,*

> *according to the tendency of the inward forces which make it a living thing.*

Personal and social liberty gives individuals the space to determine the shape of their lives for themselves, rather than having it imposed on them by state direction, social sanction, or the shackles of poverty. Individual choice also makes it more likely that people will be able actually to live their lives in the way they see fit. Liberals believe that, on the whole, people are better judges of what's in their own interest than an outside agency can be, whether that agency is government, commercial interest, or just other interfering citizens. Obviously, people sometimes make bad decisions, but so do governments; on the whole it's better to leave people to get on with things themselves.

These two elements together – deciding for oneself what is a valuable life, and successfully living one's life that way – make up what I call an ideal of individual *autonomy*. Promoting and protecting individual free choice is the best way to support people in living lives that achieve that ideal. So, in many contexts, Liberals will favour market mechanisms, precisely because they support and promote free choice. On the whole, free markets means a wider and more diverse range of options. That helps reduce the extent to which people's ideas about how they want their lives to go are constrained by a lack of options, and it increases the chances that they can exercise their freedom in a way that suits them.

As Cable notes, however, 'even the earliest economic Liberals accepted that there were important exceptions'.

Markets may be frequently be powerful tools for enhancing individual choice, and individual choice may be generally conducive to people living autonomous lives. They aren't guarantees of that, though. There are two main ways in which individual free choice – hence, markets – might fail to support our deeper ideals. First, markets won't enhance liberty if they degenerate into the sort of disastrous oligopoly that characterizes certain areas of our private sector. (In what sense, for example, does the privatized rail network offer one iota more individual choice than the nationalized British Rail that it replaced?) Second, the mere possession of a range of options, even if they're valuable, won't help individuals to lead worthwhile lives if they don't have access to full information about their options, or the wherewithal to understand that information. Under those circumstances, free choice won't help individuals at all, and in the long run the market mechanism will tend to degrade the quality of the options available, rather than enhance it.

So, Cable is right to emphasize individual choice. That emphasis must, on pain of self-defeat, go hand in hand with securing a supportive context for individual choice, so as to avoid the problems mentioned above. When assessing a proposal for private or market provision of a public service, we should therefore not only ask: does this give people greater freedom of choice? We should also ask: will this genuinely extend individual freedom of choice rather than leading to an unaccountable private monopoly or oligopoly? And will people have the information and understanding necessary to make effective use of their choices? If our answer to either question is 'no', then the proposal should be rejected. There's no justification for a market which fails to extend individual choice, even on the economic Liberal's reasoning; and there's no point in increasing individual choice without guaranteeing the background conditions which make such choice effective. In some cases, this means (as Steve Webb and Jo Holland suggest in their chapter of *The Orange Book*) that a robust education, itself free from market forces, is a precondition for the justifiability of market mechanisms being deployed elsewhere. In others – Cable mentions health as an example of this – the understanding required to make effective choices is beyond what it is reasonable to expect most citizens to possess, in which case the market mechanism can't be justified even against a robust educational background.

Alongside this suitably conditionalised concern for individual choice, I suggest a second principle, namely to show the same concern for individual *responsibility*.

As this point, many Liberal Democrats will recoil in horror. Talk of 'responsibility' in contemporary politics usually masks something distasteful and illiberal, for example the demonization of recipients of state benefits, which is merely a modern echo of old Toryish distinctions between the deserving and the undeserving poor. When it's not, it signals vacuity. (Witness David Cameron's vague appeal for an ethos of 'social responsibility' in the wake of the 2011 English riots, or Ed Milliband's contentless 'responsible capitalism' as the solution to the banking crisis.) Liberal Democrats might rightly think that the rhetoric of responsibility is only ever an attempt to disguise a lack of fresh thinking, with a tabloid-pleasing moralistic twist.

It is high time, then, to reclaim the concept of responsibility from the moralizers of both left and right. We must, because responsibility is an important component of the same ideal of autonomy which – as I suggested above – underwrites the principle of individual choice. What does it mean, we might ask, for individuals to live their lives successfully? Well, mostly it means that they are responsible for their lives: they take charge of their destiny and shape their lives as they see fit. People are responsible when their lives go well because they make it so. Therefore, a Liberal should seek to guarantee the conditions under which individuals are genuinely responsible for their lives.

Some implications of this are predictable, and sit happily with the approach of *The Orange Book*. Respect for responsibility requires, as one might expect, that the Liberal will generally favour markets, insofar as the latter also promote individual choice. When people shape their lives by making free choices, they are both exercising responsibility in forming their lives, and claiming responsibility for (at least some of) the consequences of their choices. Concern for responsibility also means reducing the extent to which people are dependent on, and their lives dominated by, overweening state power: dependency and domination both preclude true responsibility.

At the same time, respect for responsibility also places principled limits on market mechanisms. Reflecting on why reveals some important elements, absolutely central to Liberalism, which some of *The Orange Book* seems to miss.

First, merely turning a given public service over to the private or voluntary sector won't solve anything. Individuals lack responsibility for their lives if they're dependent on charity, as much as if they depend on state handouts. Responsibility is precluded by the dominance of powerful commercial interests, just as much as by state power. (Indeed, in both cases we might think that if anything there's a reason to prefer state power: at least with public provision citizens have the limited responsibility represented by democratic accountability).

Second, if we're going to take responsibility seriously by holding people responsible for the choices they make about their lives, we must also, on pain of inconsistency, seek to eliminate those factors which cause people disadvantage for reasons outwith their control. Many lives are blighted because of entrenched disadvantages for which people can't be held responsible: their family and educational backgrounds, as Webb and Holland point out; racist or sexist discrimination; lack of employment opportunities, and so on. To the extent that people's opportunities are shaped by *these* factors, rather than their own choices, they lack responsibility for their lives. If we are to show proper respect for responsibility, we must seek to eliminate these malign factors.

Third, control over one's own life is not all there is to responsibility. Another equally important element is living up to one's obligations to others in society. We all, as individuals situated in a society, have a responsibility to uphold and promote the opportunity for others to enjoy the goods which we ourselves would like to achieve. That might sound horribly onerous. How do we, as individuals, live up to such weighty obligations without them crushing any chance for us to pursue all the rich and diverse projects we want to pursue in life? Can the Liberal reconcile the need for public responsibility with scope for private autonomy? The answer is 'yes': public services, communally funded and delivered, allow us to meet those obligations in a way which leaves space for us to live our lives as we see fit in other respects. But that requires that we think about the provision of public services as part of the common good. It is in the public interest to have strong public services because it helps *all* of us: not just those who need their support at times of vulnerability, but also those of us who are liberated by the communal discharge of our individual responsibilities to each other. What remains, of course, is an individual responsibility to uphold this common good. It is important, when deciding how to deliver our public services, that the Liberal doesn't lose sight (as *The Orange Book* sometimes seems to) of the fact that they always secure an important common good, as well as providing a necessary service to different individuals at different times.

So, to summarize: alongside a principle of individual choice, we should also adopt a principle of individual responsibility, reclaiming that ill-used notion from the moralizers. This means, when assessing a proposal for private or market provision of a public service, we should ask three questions. First, does this proposal reduce dependency and domination, thereby enhancing people's responsibility for the way their lives go? Second, does it go hand in hand with measures which seek to eliminate, rather than entrench, pervasive factors which shape people's lives for reasons that lie beyond their control?

Third, does it protect the provision of public services as a common good, in all our interests? If our answer is 'no' to any of these, then we should reject the proposal. Only a woolly defender of *a la carte* Liberalism will want to adopt the rhetoric of responsibility to the extent that it apparently vindicates the free market, while ignoring the other radical commitments that concern for responsibility properly entails.

Conclusion

In this essay, I have argued that *The Orange Book* does not have a monopoly on rigorous ways to construe Liberalism, and proposed an alternative: a Liberalism based on the ideal of autonomy, that liberal citizens deserve to decide for themselves what is valuable, and to shape their lives in accordance with those decisions. This ideal motivates a concern with individual choice and with individual responsibility, and these two together generate a set of principles by which we can assess which policies a consistent Liberalism should and should not adopt. Of course, a full alternative theory of Liberalism will require considerably more argument and elucidation than I've been able to offer in this essay, and a full application of it to Liberal Democrat policy would need even more by way of detail and care. The point is just to show that it is possible to find a rigorous, consistent and tough-minded alternative to Laws's preferred emphasis on economic liberty. At the very least, this should dispel the misleading impression that *if* we are to avoid woolly thinking then we must inevitably embrace the free market. In addition, I hope it might prompt a philosophical debate within the Liberal Democrats. What better way to fight the stultification of our political imagination than by doing what we do best, and diving into radical, rigorous argument?

As I mentioned at the start, this appeal for theoretical argument might seem like self-indulgence, at a time when Liberal Democrats face such grave practical difficulties. What we should be doing is rebuilding trust, talking to voters, getting councillors elected, and trying to protect our representation in the national parliaments, not navel-gazing about abstruse questions in Liberal political theory.

I can see the reasoning behind such complaints. Nevertheless, I think them misguided, as a matter of political tactics, for three reasons.

First, one of the principal complaints levelled against the Liberal Democrats has always been that we are unprincipled opportunists, defending different policies at different times, motivated solely by short-term expediency. The best way to respond to such criticisms is to be reflective and critical as a party about the theory underpinning our policies. By showing that we have an intellectual conscience, we will be seen to be principled and consistent, as well – which is more important – as actually being those things. Maybe other parties might feel the need to pull the wool over the eyes of the voters by keeping internal discussions about principle behind closed doors. We shouldn't. We have nothing to hide, and we have much to gain from being honest.

Second: the time is ripe in British politics for more principled politics. The British public is justly and irreversibly cynical about mere spin and mood-music. What we need is new ideas, articulated clearly and honestly, to capture the public imagination, and to bring something distinctive back to Liberal Democracy. Labour and the Conservatives both seem to be trying something along these lines, with the woolly (but polychromatic) philosophies of Blue Labour and Red Toryism respectively. But we can draw upon our Liberal heritage, which contains all the greatest political thinkers of the past five hundred years. Maurice Glasman and Phillip Blond are clever, but they're no match for John Locke, Harriet Taylor, John Stuart Mill, John Maynard Keynes, and Conrad Russell. This is firm ground for us. Let other parties attack us here at their peril.

Third, and finally: the great question of our age is how to renew British politics. How should we reclaim disengaged individuals and sectors of society, and reinvigorate our battered democracy? *The Orange Book*, with its emphasis on localism, offers some good answers. I conclude with the following additional suggestion. Political thought is not something which only happens in universities, think tanks, or party policy committees. Everyone thinks about fairness, responsibility, power, and how they want their lives to go. We all constantly face questions of when to let people make their own mistakes and when to help others out. All people grapple with these political questions all the time. The tragedy of our political culture is that the practice of politics – be it in town halls, in Holyrood, in Westminster or in Brussels – has become disengaged from this vibrant everyday political thinking. We Liberal Democrats are justly proud of our experience in community politics. The logical next step in that journey is to start talking about political theory, and connecting with the political thinking that people don't realise they're doing. If it works, it will not only help to rebuild trust and electoral success at the grass roots. It will also help to save Britain from woolly thinking, and the unthinking decay of our democracy.

Chapter 4

Scotland and the United Kingdom: the Steel Commission and the independence referendum

Murray Leith

In March 2006, the Steel Commission, commissioned by the Scottish Liberal Democrats, produced its report on *Moving to Federalism - A new Settlement for Scotland* - a landmark report on the issue. The Steel Commission Report examined issues of personal and national identity, looked at the experience of federal and devolved governments in other countries, and made recommendations for the way forward, including detailed proposals for taxation powers to be exercised under a system of fiscal federalism. It examined the case for the United Kingdom and argued that the Union was of great benefit to all our constituent nations and regions. The United Kingdom, Steel stated, had been a tremendous success story for over 300 years and was bound together by many ties of common interest, history and identity. But it needed reform and modernisation along federal lines (much as had been argued by the original Scottish Commissioners of Union in 1705-6). The Scottish people then and the Scottish people now would seem to have much in common.

Subsequently, the collapse of the banks - notably the leading Scottish banks - demonstrated the level of resource which could be deployed by the United Kingdom Government to tackle such a major problem. Such resources, despite vainglorious boasts by our current First Minister, would not have been available to a separate Scottish Government with only one tenth of the resources. We are weaker apart and stronger together – as Steel made clear, the Union is greater than its constituent parts. The SNP are very aware of this which is why, as part of their plan, we are being offered independence-lite. The Queen and the Pound will stay (although this will allow any residual UK Government to deal with all the fiscal decisions linked to sterling). We will stay in the European Union - although quite why that Union is a good thing while a British Union is a bad thing has never been fully explained. It is even argued that Scottish shipyards in an independent Scotland will build ships for the Royal Navy. This talk of joint agencies and common functions only serves to confuse the issue – if we seek a partnership, we have one, surely we can mould that to suit us better rather than undergo a costly and unsure divorce?

The essence of the independence debate is whether a Scottish state, separated from the rest of the United Kingdom, meets the aspirations of people in Scotland with their various backgrounds and identities; whether Scotland will be better off or worse off under independence. Yet such comparisons – entirely proper to

banks bail out

test the independence case - are dismissed by the SNP as talking down Scotland. It is indeed gross arrogance on the part of the SNP to identify their specific party with the nation, the flag and the people. Such an approach does not allow much room for those of a different disposition. People in Scotland, in Charles Kennedy's well-known phrase, have no difficulty in identifying as Scottish (or English), British and European at the same time. Perhaps there is an even stronger identity to their region or locality, as Highlanders, Glaswegians or Aberdonians. The structures of the state should reflect these multiple identities.

The nature and structure of the British State remains one of the most significant, and ignored, problems of today. Much of the political discussion which dominates the minds and activities of key thinkers and politicians, is based on the simple fact that the UK has no written constitutional document. The current structure of the British state is a result of parliamentary decisions driven by occasional violent demands, political decisions of party leaders at various points in time, and only recently, endorsed by popular sentiment through public referenda, a new innovation in British politics. Referenda are a populist and emotional means of achieving constitutional change that is suspect in the eyes of many, and specifically outlawed in many leading democracies.

As a state without a written constitution, the UK operates along principles laid down over time, contained within a variety of documents and legislation, and judicial decisions; but these can be changed at political whim, by majorities of the moment, with no consideration for the long term implications or ramifications beyond the immediate decision and focus. Scottish devolution (and the devolution decisions for Wales, and Northern Ireland) is, in some respects, a classic example of just such a decision; a decision made and implemented through statute within a matter of months. Yet, strangely enough, the argument and fight for devolved powers in Scotland was not new.

A century of talking

About one hundred years ago the nature and structure of the British political system was also the subject of much discussion at Westminster and within the public sphere. Bills to provide home rule, or devolution, to Ireland, Scotland and Wales, all with varying powers and authorities, were proposed and discussed in the House of Commons. A Speaker's Committee was convened to discuss the issues, but nought came of that. In the end, the seismic implications of World War I, the depression of the 1920s and 1930s, and then Word War II, headed off such considerations. Pulling together, the people of Britain, and the wider Empire, fought for freedom and democracy as a United Kingdom.

Yet it should be no surprise to anyone that Scotland, as a people and a nation, consistently returned to the issue of Home Rule and in the 1970s and, after the defeat of home rule bills in Westminster, the debate continued until a Scottish parliament came into being in 1999. In many respects, it had simply been a matter of time. In every decade since the beginning of the 20th Century (and with much prior activity too) a movement, association, or political party was created to drive devolution forward and greater democracy would only strengthen the outcome.

The arrival of mass politics in Scotland served to highlight the wish of the Scottish people to have a greater say over their own affairs albeit within the United Kingdom . The Scottish Parliament exists because of the will of the Scottish people. This is evident from such movements as the Scottish Home Rule Association of the 1920s, the Scottish Convention of the 1940s and the Scottish Covenant of the 1950s, where over a million plus individuals publicly committed themselves, in writing, to the idea of a devolved Scottish parliament. Yet, like many such appeals, it fell on deaf ears as the two major parties of British politics ignored such pleas in favour of their own objectives. The will of the people of Scotland was thwarted by the political elite of Britain. Such actions led to the Scottish people turning to other political parties – Nationalists and Liberals alike. This is why Liberals and Liberal Democrats have been Home Rulers for over a century, and played a major part both in designing the scheme for a Scottish Parliament and in ensuring consensus for its principles across a broad swath of Scottish civic and political life. We have been central among the voices calling for home rule, just as we played a solid part in the civic and political actions that helped shape and deliver the current parliament; a claim that the SNP cannot make. Liberals and Liberal Democrats have always realised that devolution – which we prefer to see as Home Rule – in Scotland could not be a stand alone process.

The current situation in Scotland is one of demands for greater decentralisation of political authority and powers from Westminster, mixed with demands from the Scottish Nationalists for separation and Scottish independence. The nature of the devolved political system and our electoral system has delivered the Nationalists a majority of seats (albeit on a minority of votes) and sole control of the parliament itself. Their demands for separation, full, 'lite' or limited, depending upon the day, co-exist with the recognition by other political parties that Holyrood does need greater powers. Such a position was forcefully presented by the Steel Commission – well before the political rise of the current SNP administration. Home rule as part of a federal UK is our goal and it is the goal of the majority of the Scottish people today.

It is in this mixture of Nationalist political control, and general popular support for greater powers, a heady brew indeed, that Scotland faces a choice for her future. Yet in almost every political poll taken during the latter part of the 20th century, and during these years of devolution itself, only one or two polls have ever indicated that a majority of Scots seek to separate themselves from their British cousins. The vast majority indicate that those that do represent at best about a third of the population. While this may be a minority, any student of history can tell you this is more than enough to drive a separation movement in the right circumstances. Many leading academics have pointed out that such circumstances may now be upon us, as there exists an urgent need to consider the UK level implications of devolution, so that a settled structure can be imposed, and that popular or political forces cannot drive the discussion properly in the absence of that structure.

What structure do we need today?

What we require for Scotland, as part of the UK, is a formal and clear UK constitution, a constitution that enshrines federalism at the core of the British State and provides the UK, and its constituent members, with clear authority, powers and responsibilities through their own, national and regional constitutions. It is through the very absence of such documents that we find ourselves in the difficult and precarious times of today. The lack of a written constitution not only stirs populist challenges from within the political system, it also means we lack a formal method by which we can change the system! At a time when unemployment is reaching levels unseen in this generation, so many of our office holders are spending their time and strength on arguing the case for who has the authority (moral or political, although as a Liberal Democrat I have often considered them to be inseparable) to hold a referendum on the dissolution of the Union. There is no doubt that this is an important matter, but greater and more immediate concerns exist. Home Rule allows Scottish solutions to Scottish problems, but the problems of Scotland are lost amid a debate about what the future of Scotland should be. The stirring of emotion and the inflammation of passion is not conducive to a calm-headed and detailed consideration of what status Scotland should have in the future, at a time when the immediate present and future looks bleak for 231,000 unemployed Scots.

Simply put, the lack of a written constitution is a problem that the UK has not addressed, and it is one that the country must consider if it is to survive as a political entity in the 21st Century. The issue is encapsulated in the argument surrounding the (re)arising of the West Lothian Question in Westminster today. The popular wish of many Conservative MPs is to bring about English Votes for English Laws (or EVEL), or to reduce the number of MPs sitting from the devolved nations. Both these 'solutions' contain within them considerable implications that will, not might, bring about ill will and bad feeling from citizens right across the United Kingdom. Cutting the number of Scottish MPs, or limiting their ability to vote in the Parliament that remains the sovereign assembly of the UK could only provoke matters further and provide succour to those seeking to dissolve the Union. Yet there is another solution, an English Parliament, within a federal UK.

The immediate reaction to this solution is simple in its form. After all, if Scotland has a parliament, and Wales and Northern Ireland each have an Assembly, why not England? But that is to point to the unbalanced nature of such a Union. The so called problem is that England has roughly 85% of the population, and several individuals have consistently questioned how does one maintain such an unbalanced, asymmetrical devolution or lop-sided federalism? Of course, the Union has existed with population imbalance for over 300 years, but it is a question which bears reflection and requires addressing.

Many unions, federal in nature, exist around the world, and again, the Steel Commission discussed the implications for such a Union. It provided 22 clear recommendations that would allow Scotland to be part of a more federal UK. The issues address the implication of fiscal control, as well as providing means to address issues such as international relations and defence within a federated UK. Furthermore, population imbalances can be found within such diverse federal unions as the US – where California makes up 12.1% of the House of Representative with 53 Congressional Representatives, while Montana has just 1. Population imbalance requires careful consideration, but does not of itself provide grounds for rejection of a federal solution.

The situation facing Scotland, and the UK, in the second decade of devolution is clear evidence of the need for a constitution. Putting aside the arguments and challenges surrounding the issue of separation and the powers that Scotland should gain within the Union, there are clear and immediate needs that our political system requires and which a written constitution would provide. A formal system would provide safeguards against the passion of the moment and changes that suit political factions rather than the nation as a whole. The ability of a system to withstand populist challenges is not guaranteed by the presence of a constitution, as a history of the 20th century so eloquently illustrates, but *having* a constitution, *adhering* to that constitution, and *operating within it* does. Furthermore, a constitution would not only provide clear demarcation between the duties and responsibilities of the state, and those of the nation, but it would also provide for those of the citizen.

A way forward for the 21st century

Scotland has long operated as a nation of individuals bound together within the territory that is Scotland. We have derived our strength by accepting individuals within that territory as fellow Scots. When other nations had Kings of the land, we had a King of the people – King of Scots, not King of Scotland. In our modern times this has translated into the idea that sovereignty comes from the people, and that it is only in the name of the people that a government can operate and serve. A constitution would enshrine such principles for today and tomorrow. As individuals within Scotland we need to know our rights and responsibilities, so that we can ensure that just as the state carries out its duties to us, we ensure we meet our responsibilities to the nation and to each other.

The case for Home Rule within a reformed and more federal United Kingdom is a modern, inclusive and optimistic one, suited to the needs of the 21st century, and wholly in the interests of Scotland. By contrast, the case for national independence is an old fashioned and divisive one, which narrows Scotland's horizons and opportunities, and the contribution that we can make to the world.

Chapter 5

Effectiveness in the public sector

John Aldridge

A frequently peddled mantra on the right, supported by the so called "markets" (really just a large number of selfish and irrational speculators), is: "private sector good; public sector bad". This is reinforced by traditional economic theory, which states that spending on public services "squeezes out" beneficial private investment. They've never explained satisfactorily what the difference is in practical terms and in the effect on the nation's economy between a hospital, a school or a prison built with public finance and one built with private finance. Both are pre-empting resources which could be used for other purposes – in the case of the privately financed institution, other things being equal, rather more resources are pre-empted (since Governments can generally borrow money more cheaply than the private sector). Economists would argue that relying on the private sector means that there is no distortion to priorities which happens when the public sector is involved. But that assumes that political priorities should be subordinate to economic ones – a dubious proposition to say the least.

But the parallel left wing mantra - "public sector good, private sector bad" - is equally false. The fact is that, in many areas of civic life, the private sector can and does provide good quality services often spurred on by the goad of competition, an established Liberal principle. And of course, however financed, it will be private sector companies that actually build the facilities, and provide many of the support services that keep them running.

But there are problems with relying on the private sector. In a capitalist economy there is an inevitable tendency towards monopoly. This is because the most efficient and cheapest supplier will drive less efficient and more expensive suppliers out of business. In practice this doesn't always happen, but there is a need for the state to regulate areas of public life where monopoly is developing. On the whole, if a service is in effect a monopoly, it is easier and cheaper to regulate it in the public sector than in the private sector. A current example of this is the UK railway system. The track owner is Network Rail – a monopoly – and services are provided almost exclusively by local monopoly franchises. This system's regulation requires extraordinarily complex and expensive arrangements. For all its faults, the nationalised BR was a lot easier and cheaper to regulate, as are the still largely nationalised European railway systems.

So there is no simple answer to the question of whether public sector or private sector is better. And there will always be a substantial public sector which needs to be subject to checks and controls to ensure it is operating as it should. Over the years Governments have introduced various measures to try to achieve this aim. They have included requiring the public sector to:

- pass "Value for Money" tests;

- compulsorily put services out to tender;

- test for "Best Value";

- benchmark services against comparators.

Underlying all of these approaches has been the pursuit of the "3Es" – economy, efficiency and effectiveness. Broadly speaking, "economy" means getting services as cheaply as possible; "efficiency" is about getting more for the same amount of money, or the same level of service for less money; "effectiveness" is about getting the best possible quality of service within whatever financial constraints are in force.

In a time of austerity, economy is always important, and indeed a lot of the comparison work that goes on – competitive tendering for example – is focussed on reducing cost. Efficiency has become overused by politicians who claim to be able to detect "inefficiency" and waste in the public sector, and to be able to eliminate it. The pursuit of effectiveness often gets lost in the squabbles about improving efficiency.

But, achieving the best possible public services needs a balance to be struck between the 3 Es. With the concentration on economy and efficiency this is rarely done. Economy is of course desirable, but simply cutting costs – especially when it has to be done at short notice –

is likely to lead to indiscriminate reductions in both good and bad services. Furthermore, public services tend to be labour intensive, and cuts in them tend to fall disproportionately on staff numbers. That in turn leads to higher costs for the economy as a whole in unemployment and other support, and increases stress levels on those staff still employed, whose workload increases. Public services are often demand led, meaning that the number of clients dealt with cannot be easily controlled. Indeed, when attempts are made to do so, for example by instituting waiting lists for non-emergency medical treatment, there is an enormous public outcry. The medium to long term effects of increased stress include burn out, higher sickness absence, and an unhappy workforce, particularly dangerous in caring professions.

The pursuit of efficiency shares many of the risks associated with economy. But there is also a fundamental flaw if it is taken to its logical end. An absolutely efficient service has no spare capacity – all its resources are being used at all times. First this means that there is no place for competition, since competition requires the client or service user to be able to choose between options, and if that choice is available, when the user picks one option, the other is redundant. That means resources are not all used, and therefore there is inefficiency. In addition, seeking to ensure public services operate at their maximum efficiency does not allow for unexpected emergencies. Trauma hospitals need to be able to cope with a major road accident for example. If all the hospital beds are always full (and therefore operating at maximum efficiency) they would not be able to deal with such eventualities. Furthermore, efficiency could be increased in schools by the simple expedient of increasing class sizes, but it is unlikely that that would be welcomed.

Effectiveness is the orphan child of the three. Pursuing effectiveness always seems to be the last of the three to be addressed, although it is often the aspect of most interest to service users. It is of course not possible to pursue effectiveness at all costs. Quality can always be improved, but the cost of doing so can be disproportionate. However, that is no justification for concentrating on cost and efficiency at the expense of effectiveness.

So what practical approach should be taken by Liberals? First, it is vital that the pursuit of effectiveness is more emphasised so that there is a better balance between it and the other two Es. Some options for developing the public sector have included:

- reorganisation of public sector bodies

- a performance target regime

- more reliance on the third sector.

Each of these will be considered in turn. It is to the credit of all Scottish administrations since devolution that they have avoided launching serial reorganisations of local authorities or health boards, while south of the border, the equivalent organisations have had to cope with constant organisational change. That is not to say that reorganisation is never warranted. The Wheatley Commission in the 1970s analysed carefully the various powers of local authorities, and concluded that they could be split into strategic and more local services. That analysis is still surprisingly robust, although local government structure was changed to a unitary arrangement from the Regions and Districts which flowed from Wheatley. But both of these more recent structures are much better than the hotchpotch that preceded them.

However, one lesson which has emerged from the limited reorganisations in Scotland and from the more frequent and disruptive ones in England is that there is no perfect structural answer. Any new structure may solve some apparent problems but will create new ones. And the cost of undertaking the reorganisation can often outweigh any practical benefits. It is often argued that reducing the number of public bodies will increase efficiency. That may not necessarily be true. If the same work still has to be done, it is likely that virtually the same number of people will be needed to do it. And simply operating two functions in the same organisation does not necessarily get rid of the boundaries between them.

More significantly, the larger the organisation, the more remote it is likely to be, or at least feel, from its clients. This raises the whole issue of localism versus centralisation, and is a good exemplification of the tension between efficiency and effectiveness. It can be argued that, at least in theory, a single central organisation providing a public service like health, education, or policing is the most efficient configuration. But it is much more doubtful whether it is the most effective approach. In terms of economy, a single organisation would save the cost of chief executive officers. As far as efficiency is concerned, it *ought* to be possible to coordinate activity more successfully, and to ensure a standard level of service. But in terms of effectiveness, there is likely to be a loss of local knowledge and sensitivity; and by providing a standard level of service the scope for local variation to meet local needs would be reduced, as would the scope for new thinking. One of the most overused, tired and insidious terms prevalent in modern life in Scotland is the designation of any variation in service as "a post code lottery". Where such variation is the result of a deliberate act, it is not a lottery. And without allowing for variations to meet local needs and to try new approaches any public service will stagnate. Those who argue for centralised services are, wittingly or not, supporting such stagnation.

Many Governments have introduced performance target regimes to try to improve public services. The first thing to be clear about is that targets work. Although often unpopular with the professionals who are charged with meeting the targets, where they have been applied – for example in reducing waiting times for hospital treatment – they have achieved their objective. What they do not do, however, is to achieve a general improvement in public services. Achievement of the target takes precedence over other activity, and as the target is met, public concern moves on to other aspects of the service, which have often been relatively neglected in the dash to meet the target.

The role of the third sector in relation to public services has changed over the years. Traditionally charities operated as gadflies, pestering the public service providers to improve what they provide, and providing specialist services on a small scale where the general public provider could or would not provide it. The third sector has been praised for its ability to react quickly to changing needs, and to provide high quality specialist and individually tailored services more cheaply than larger suppliers, partly because they can call on committed volunteers. That has led to them being looked to to provide more and more services, which in turn has led some parts of the charitable third sector to become more commercial in their outlook. Some in that sector argue that because they are increasingly taking over the provision of services previously delivered by the public sector they should be paid the same. That is a very dangerous argument. As they become bigger charitable service providers lose the spontaneity and fleetness of foot that gives them the edge in terms of the quality of services. And combining that with an erosion of their cost advantage will lead to their use in providing public services being called into question.

The third sector also includes cooperatives and other non-profit making organisations. The Coalition Government's avowed support for cooperatives to be established to take over the provision of some public services has much merit. But it will only work if they are given some protection from unfair competition from the private sector, so that they can remain small and flexible organisations like the best of the charities, and still get the service contracts.

So, in the light of this, what approach should be taken to move towards a Liberal vision of public services?

- It should be driven by a determination to pursue the effectiveness of services at least as much as their efficiency and economy.

- There should be a preference for local and flexible services rather than centralised and monolithic ones

- There should be no hang ups about whether the services are provided by the public, private or third sectors, but each should be judged against the criterion of effectiveness

- Competition should be encouraged, particularly in terms of encouraging small scale flexible and responsive suppliers to show how services can be improved

- Charitable third sector organisations should not be required to become pseudo commercial enterprises to play their part in delivering public services.

There is a window of opportunity to bring about the change of emphasis set out above. For the next three or four years, public spending is going to be shrinking in real terms. Budgets for all public services will be cut, and judgements will have to be made as to where the cuts fall. That should be an opportunity to focus the cuts on the least efficient and effective services. However, that is unlikely to happen in reality. Instead, the Scottish and UK Governments will largely spread the misery more or less equally, because to do otherwise would stir up enormous criticism from interest groups.

However, when available public spending starts growing again, probably in about 2016, Liberals should argue for the new additional resources to be directed to where they will be most effective in bringing about the aims above. In short, effectiveness, not just efficiency should be our guide.

Chapter 6

Community Power, Community Wealth Creation and the New Localism

Denis Robertson Sullivan

If we had been asked to define one of our key aims as Liberal Democrats we might well have used terms like "community empowerment", "people power" or "localism". We instinctively feel and know that arrangements where people make decisions about their own lives themselves – or failing that have them decided at a level as near to their communities as possible - makes sense.

Indeed subsidiarity is a good Liberal Democrat principle for all governmental institutions from Europe down to local Councils and beyond. Devolving power to the most local level increases the opportunity for individuals to make a difference, and thus tends to increase engagement with society. As Ben Colburn notes earlier in this book, "context is all".

We should prefer action by the affected community itself rather than national state action itself — local councils and municipal authorities tend to produce measures that are more imaginative and better suited to the daily reality of a social problem.

Indeed, since the 1970s, a whole method of political campaigning – some would say a philosophy – has been built by the Party on community campaigning and our hallmark "Focus" leaflets. Liberal Democrats rightly have a strong reputation as local champions, and for identifying, seizing, campaigning and acting on local grievances.

It is arguable, however, that, despite many individual successes, the rhetoric has sometimes been more powerful than the reality when Liberal Democrats have obtained control or leadership positions on local councils. There have been significant efforts in the direction of devolving to and empowering area committees and some new ideas about engaging the public, but the end result is still growing apathy by many people about the relevance of party politics, disinterest in local politics and perhaps a decay in the concept of community politics itself.

More broadly, the idea of localism has been seen at various times in different ways:

- as an important component of the environmental movement – "think global, act local", the use of concepts like food miles to recreate more local supply chains, the Schumacher "small is beautiful" concept

- as an archaic, conservative concept, harking back to pre-industrialisation days when personal relationships were on a more local basis

- as a dynamic democratic force, where social enterprises, co-operatives and local credit unions for example are seen as ways to release community dynamic

The Coalition Government has recently passed the Localism Act 2011 (which applies primarily only to England and Wales) as provided for in the Coalition Agreement. Its avowed aim is to "promote the radical devolution of power and greater financial autonomy to local government and community groups", but it certainly does not do what it says on the tin. Arguably its only significant community empowerment measure is contained in Section 81 which requires Local Authorities to consider "expressions of interest" by community groups in running specific council services. I deliberately exclude the proposal to give residents the power to instigate local referenda on any local issue and the power to veto excessive tax increases – which seem to me to be a classic example of power – or apparent power – without responsibility, and a negation of liberal democracy.

However the debates around the Bill raised some other interesting issues. What is meant by localism and community empowerment? How far is local empowerment a "Nimby's Charter"? What is a postcode lottery and what is flexibility in local decision making? And, of course, many people have questioned whether David Cameron's concept of the "Big Society" has any real substance to it.

There are other challenges – in some cases, local power elites can be as authoritarian as national ones. How can we have true and effective accountability?

Further, rich localities start with advantages of education and power over poor localities. How can we avoid poorer communities being disadvantaged further, other than by action by the state?

And, despite the undoubted successes of Social Inclusion Partnerships and Community Planning in some areas, it is true to say that the community and public involvement in many of these structures is woefully ineffective.

Let me explore a few ideas on whether the idea of community empowerment is valid, what the obstacles are, and how might they be overcome.

Community Engagement – People

Liberal Democrats believe in local empowerment - indeed it speaks to the heart of what we believe - but how loudly do we say it and how do we explain it or describe it?

For many of us, local and community empowerment could be the dynamo of a fresh influx of strength to our democracy. Local institutions and loyalties are still hugely powerful – the identity of the old Burghs and Royal Burghs, the strength of community bodies, clubs and voluntary groups. The institutions of Government must recognise and use these building blocks – indeed we know municipalities and communes are the bulwark of successful democracy in many parts of Europe.

What is the outcome we seek to achieve? It is that we want more people to be engaged or involved in running their own communities and their organisations, for their own benefit and for the benefit of the community. A win-win situation.

We believe that the more individuals invest in their communities, then the more they will value it and benefit from it. The more individuals participate in our society at every level and especially locally, then the stronger our democracy will be, since involvement is the building block of communities.

But we are painfully aware too that many local organisations fail to reach the potential they are capable of.

The effectiveness of community councils is hugely variable, and this is probably related to their relative lack of power, resources and professional staff, and the lack of contested elections to them – compared for example to English Town Councils or indeed Housing Associations which have both resource and the support of professional staff.

Many sports clubs – despite the publicity boon of the London Olympics and the Glasgow Commonwealth Games – cater to a declining or ageing membership or have assets such as club houses which sit unused for much of the time.

Many community organisations are staffed by the well-meaning efforts of a small number of overstretched individuals who sit on too many committees – and many fail entirely to attract the necessary dynamism or the expertise which exists in most local communities.

On the other hand, there are some notable success stories. The community-based Housing Associations are one – often innovative and dynamic, both in housing and in wider action terms. Many nursery groups are the hubs for a buzz of other activities; some community halls or bases house a critical mass of active, thrusting organisations which are mutually sustaining; some community campaigns like the Govanhill Pool Campaign instil a unique flavour which puts them above more limited protest groups.

We need to recognise the diversity of organisations that sustain local communities. We need to bottle success and, if possible duplicate it. What are the best ways to empower and grow them? How can we ensure they are as flexible and as responsive as they are diverse? Franchise successful community groups!

We need to engage more people into the process too. All community organisations are run by people, but, in my experience, the running is usually left to a tiny pool of people in all organisations to do the work – the activists. Undoubtedly there are potential pools of other people with abilities who could be tapped into to assist in building up community empowerment - the existing inactive members, the unemployed and the non-employed. Let us think creatively how this might be done.

We need too to rethink the way in which voluntary groups are supported. Arguably there has been relative over-investment in national structures and under-investment in regional and local support. Some organisations are well capable of supporting their local units and delivering high quality, consistent, and well monitored standards. Examples such as Scottish Scouting or Citizens' Advice Scotland come to mind. The need here is to invest in headquarters support and training to enable them to grow, not to impose extra layers of national or local inspection or red tape on them.

But other organisations may exist only in one locality and might benefit from a locally available and tailored support in developing business plans or growing their service. Different, more local support is needed.

The problem of resources

The current financial crisis hits the Third Sector with a double whammy – a reduced pot of funding from both public and private sources, and a greater need for services.

Let us start by recognising that we live in a land of shrinking budgets. We must be in the business of working smarter, more efficiently and effectively and of recognising the huge potential resource there is in people. There might be some money round the edges, perhaps additional cash from the Big Lottery. The Big Lottery has indeed done well in facilitating new methods of community engagement and we should encourage them to spend more money on even more community empowerment.

Sensible co-location of certain public and voluntary sector services, more sharing of support services like payroll, inventive approaches such as the idea of payment

by results which is being trialled in prison aftercare –
areas like this may yield up resources for reallocation.

But both central and local government need to give
greater priority, even within constrained resources, to
resourcing effective community and voluntary
organisations. We should, for example, look at ways in
which the local community might receive more directly
the rewards of what is going on in their area.

This idea has already made some progress in the
development of community windfarms and of district
heating schemes which produce energy and revenue for
local communities and local causes. Energy is perhaps
one of the most buoyant of potential revenue sources for
local communities. There are also parallels in the landfill
tax which has supported various local causes.

Councils often benefit from planning gain from
significant developments in their areas, but there can be
considerable dissatisfaction with what may itself be a
controversial development, and with the opaque methods
of deciding and disposing of the windfall from the
planning gain. Despite the immediate temptations for the
council to claw in the money, it may well make sense to
allow a local community to benefit directly through its
local organisations from some or all of the resource.

The same is true of industrial or housing
developments - could there not be a method of obtaining
payment into a Local Community Fund from developers,
or from the sale of land in their areas? In this way, change
of land use would bring very localised community gain,
as well as gains to the wider community. This would
greatly change a local community's views on local

development, especially if they could see some direct and tangible local benefit rather than some amorphous "wider-community" benefit. We should look at ways to bring the rewards more directly to those who live with the changes and the businesses in their community.

There are also governmental organisations and funded enterprises whose resources could be more targeted at this objective – like the Local Authorities, the Health Boards, Quangos, or indeed those in receipt of substantial sums of Government support such as Housing Associations. Most Housing Associations have significant capital balances. Of course these are needed to pay for ongoing rehabilitation and for current maintenance. Nevertheless, subject to suitable guarantees, these resources could be tapped into to underwrite and support future and much-needed housing and other investment in local communities. An idea for future discussion might be a Government or public interest "Golden Share" where grants and support are given which result in the creation of assets – assets which can then be put against borrowing or otherwise support investment. It is a concept which both the UK and the Scottish Government have been examining.

Community Power

We need to be open to a structure and ethos of Local Government that encourages the devolution of its power to those who can and should have it. We should start by looking at the models of devolved authority which are working most effectively in Local Government and then ask ourselves how do we adopt and grow these examples across our Local Authorities – Franchise Local Devolution!

There is no perfect structure of local government and no one wants a further wholesale reorganisation of council boundaries. However, many Local Authorities are an amalgamation of old Burghs that once ruled themselves. Why cannot we start there – with those who want or would accept control of their own affairs and give them back some of the power over their own areas. This is not a mantra of imposition but one of encouraging independence and responsibility; handing back to those who can handle it and want it - encouraging more communities to take on more. We should seek to create a genuinely pluralist approach to localism – encourage, facilitate and not dictate, in which some areas may choose to manage their libraries or handle dealing with graffiti or street cleanliness or whatever while others do not. Our instincts should be to devolve and to encourage it.

But such responsible local communities need appropriate funding and dynamic, robust bodies accountable to them in order to undertake such responsibilities. We need to give as much effort to developing successful models as we do to other priorities.

One part of the jigsaw of dynamic communities can be provided by co-operatives and social enterprises. I want to reclaim the title of social enterprise for organisations which make surpluses and do not need continued financial support. I want to encourage our Local Authorities and the Scottish Government to build up and grow the funds available to new and emerging

Social Enterprises committed to making surpluses. It is important to stress that this investment is in social enterprises that are designed and planned on the basis that they will be self-sufficient and make surpluses (profits) to be reinvested.

By growing this form of Social Enterprise we create employment and economic activity and the benefits of efforts of those involved goes back into the business or community they serve. We should be actively encouraging this kind of job creation and enterprise especially in these straitened times. Organisations like the Prince's Trust are very well experienced in this area and we should seek to partner with them and Scottish Business in the Community and Scottish Enterprise in order to ensure the social enterprises invested in, have strong business plan and good mentoring support during their gestation and growth periods.

One of the themes Liberal Democrats should be developing is that of rebuilding economic and social organisations on a more local, community and human scale.

Community Land Rights

Scots law contains the ancient but fertile doctrine of "common good". Common good land is essentially land held by the former Burghs for the common good of their inhabitants – or property or assets purchased with the proceeds of their sale. By and large, the reformed Councils responsible for common good property have not been good custodians of it – nor always were the old Burghs themselves. The land reformer, Andy Wightman, has done a lot of work to lay the foundations for modernising the concept of common good. It is something Scottish Liberal Democrats should commit to – with the aim of safeguarding community assets and creating a sustainable and inalienable community land bank.

We must escape from a narrow concept of the ownership of land. The idea that someone or some organisation owns land in some kind of totally unfettered way is absurd. Land exists in a community; it gains its value by being in or near communities - so the community should have some rights over it too. Why is it we tolerate the underdevelopment or poor development of land in communities which are hugely impacted by what goes on, or does not go on, on that very land, in their communities – where are the community's rights? If land lies vacant in their area, why do they not have "community rights" over it so they can insist that something is done with it?

Our cities and communities are blighted by ugly derelict land – and indeed unused empty houses - that makes the community look bad and encourages a sense of abandonment. How many streetscapes are blighted by empty and abandoned shops? Why does a farmer benefit from change of land use, but not the local community whose land it is in? Why do they not see direct benefit? Why is it that developers can bank land until the land grows in value and they then realise the improved value – why do the very local communities not also get a share of that improvement? They live in the area; they create the community within which the land exists. This is a longstanding Liberal theme (and one amplified in Ross Finnie's advocacy of land value taxation in his essay) -

why do the local people then not share in the advantages created by the communities they create round that land?

For many communities, what is done with the land in their community is a great determinant of what happens in and to that community, so this land and power relationship has to be re-examined.

Temporary Re-Use

We should not allow the banking of land at no cost. Where land, housing or a shop lies vacant and unused, we should insist it is kept in good repair or given the opportunity of community use. The cost of maintenance should be a lien on the property, repayable when it is sold. There are practical difficulties to be overcome such as the problem of contaminated land, but the principle is clear. There are huge financial opportunities for very local communities with what is proposed here, but I am also keen to see that land and shops are not left abandoned to blight the local community. We should insist that any land or vacant sites and shops must be developed within a set period of time (three, five or ten years?) failing which the land owner loses a proportion of the land for every year of underdevelopment to that very local community to pay for its community use upkeep.

Further we should insist that even small sites are not left to rot and become ugly blots, defacing the communities that have to live with them. We should insist that there is a "green local community" use to that land awaiting development or redevelopment. Such land should be turned over to small parks, meadows, allotments, play areas, parking or whatever - and that should be done by negotiation with the local community itself, whilst they await re/development.

Accepting that any such enhancement might only be temporary (though I know several near city centre locations that have lain temporarily abandoned and rotting for what turned out to be decades), temporary re-use would not or should not erode the owner's entitlement to develop later. The community could seek to have land "reclaimed" if a factory was abandoned or is falling down. Imagine if a community could "acquire" the land through a non-use or non-utilisation legal provision in the planning regulations. This would give local communities a right either to redevelop the land or knock the factory down and recover their costs for doing so from the owner or simply take ownership of the land and factory and then demolish or redevelop.

Public Organisations and their Properties and their Land

Let me take but one example – schools. Instead of charging parents and the community to use schools, what if that local community had negotiated the right to use of the facility for a certain number of hours a year in the area surrounding the school before the school was built?

It may be that to have a school, a community would have to agree to look after the playing fields and that could be done by a very local service level agreement. If the community failed to live up to its side of the bargain, then the agreement of use falls or funds might be drawn down from their Local Community Fund to pay for the short coming of the service.

A New Partnership and Approach

If we really believe in empowering people/communities, we need to change the way we think about communities and how we deal with them and stop governing them but see government as a consensual activity that needs cooperation and responsibility to be a shared experience. I have chosen only schools but every community is full of buildings and land paid for by the "public" or in which there is a "public subsidy" but where some centralised or independent body has "control" over it.

Why is it that Housing Associations do not automatically have "local community representatives on their boards as well as tenants?" Governments put very large sums of money into Housing Associations. Why is it tenants who have primacy in their organisations (by and large albeit not exclusively) and not a full representation of the community too? Why does Government not retain some percentage of ownership right to the housing or land, so recognising its contribution to building costs? We could describe it as a Government "golden share".

I want Liberal Democrats to take ownership of Localism, to learn from those who do it well and to challenge ourselves to devolve more power. I want us to think differently about land ownership and entitlement. I want us to think differently how we raise taxes and disburse them and how we grow community wealth. Indeed, local and community empowerment could be the dynamo of a fresh influx of strength to our democracy.

Scotland and the UK have suffered successively from Thatcherite greed and Labour bossiness and of the State knowing best. It is time to replace these by a Liberal Democrat stress on people – on the individual, on the family and on the community. This should be at the heart of our philosophy.

Chapter 7

The crisis of Ethics – the failure of leadership

Elspeth Attwooll

The better and fairer distribution of wealth; the concession to the active producer of a more adequate share of the product of his labour, which is but another way of expressing the demand for a "living wage"; the shortening of hours of labour – are questions which touch very closely, not only the lives of our industrial millions, but the national life itself.

So wrote W Kinnaird Rose in a book entitled *The Liberal Platform* and published in 1895.

Well over a century later, these questions are far from resolved. Why is it that, in the UK, full time employees spend longer at work than anywhere else in the EU but achieve less than average productivity? Why is it that there are still such differences in income between various sectors of society – bankers, quango bosses and football stars (to name but some) on the one hand and factory workers, those providing services and (mostly) members of the caring professions on the other? Why, too, is it that, more than 30 years after the Equal Pay Act, women in full time employment still earn on average 15.5% less than men? How come that the UK boasts more than one and a half million children in poverty – 17,000 of them in Glasgow alone? And that a million under 25s are unemployed – whilst the pension age is being raised for the older generation?

None of this squares with the Liberal Democrat commitment in the Preamble to the Party Constitution:

> *To build and safeguard a fair, free and open society, in which we seek to balance out the fundamental values of liberty, equality and community, and in which no one shall be enslaved by poverty, ignorance or conformity....*

Apart from the eight years of partnership government in Scotland, where the ending of tuition fees and the introduction of free personal care for the elderly reflected this commitment – we have not been in a position of power for some considerable time. So it might seem unfair to lay any of the blame for the situation at our own door. Yet we can still ask how far our policies are attuned to our commitments and, more directly, question the extent to which the coalition is serving them.

One can, of course point to the raising of the tax threshold, the introduction of the pupil premium in England and steps to combat youth unemployment, as well as various other measures, but, when looked at in the round, it seems that efforts to tackle the financial deficit are still bearing hardest on those who already have the least. The recent projection of another 400,000 children falling into poverty over the next five years does not augur well for the values of liberty, equality and community. Nor does it fit with the claim of the liberal philosopher, John Rawls, that 'justice as fairness requires that all primary social goods be distributed equally unless an unequal distribution would be to everyone's advantage'. Of which, more later.

The projection itself, though, raises the whole question of just how current conditions have arisen. To those of us who completed our education in the sixties, the prospects looked fair. The great majority of us did not anticipate problems in finding employment and most of us expected to be in the same occupation until we retired. Technological developments seemed to imply that this would be earlier rather than later and that during our working lives we would have shorter hours and longer holidays. A concession to longer holidays apart, the reverse has been the case.

It would take a detailed analysis of the last fifty years or so of economic history to determine just why this has happened. But one thing does seem to be apparent. Over the course of them we have moved into what is very much a consumer society. To put matters more crudely, to a mentality of "must have it and must have it now", where the 'it' is constantly changing.

We are told that vast salaries and bonuses for bankers and moguls of industry are necessary to keep their expertise in operation and that a 50p tax rate on the higher paid is stifling for business. The average earnings of the top ten percent of the population is twelve times that of the bottom ten percent and, according to an OECD Report in 2011, the gap between rich and poor is said to be increasing faster than that in any other wealthy country.

Yet our commitment in the Preamble to our Constitution is that:

> ....*We will foster a strong and sustainable economy which encourages the necessary wealth creating processes, develops the skills of people and works to the benefit of all, with a just distribution of the rewards of success.*

We find, too, that the current financial deficit at national level is mirrored by the personal one. Our average household debt is estimated at £60,000 when mortgages are included and, even more a concern, £10,000 when they are not. The words of Mr Micawber: 'Annual income twenty pounds, annual expenditure nineteen and six, result happiness. Annual expenditure twenty pounds ought and six, result misery" are no less true than they were in Dickens' time – it is just that the effects may take longer to be felt.

This is not of itself to decry institutions such as mortgages and hire purchase or investments in companies. It is only to signal the dangers when the former are engaged in irresponsibly by lenders or borrowers or both and to issue a reminder that playing the stock exchange is a form of gambling like (or perhaps unlike) any other. It is also to question the desirability of financial markets controlling political decisions rather than the other way round. It is only too obvious at present just how far this has become the case. Obviously, in a mixed economy, almost any government action will have effects in the monetary world and these need to be taken into account but, when governments only allow themselves to do what they believe that world will endorse, there must be some cause for concern.

Nor is it just financial markets that may be at play in engendering political decisions. The media, too, can have a major role – particularly when they create or reinforce moral panics. Immigration might be cited as a case in point. There is, too, the extent to which the decision-makers themselves are overly motivated by what they believe to be the desires of that part of the electorate that supports them or those of their own constituents. Hence the recent plea that MPs should forbear simply to defend their local hospital when doing so may not be in the best interests of the NHS as a whole.

This leads in to the whole issue of leadership. In the current context one might define an effective leader as someone who either creates a political tide or swims hard against the prevailing one, in both cases taking his or her supporters along. F W de Klerk and the ending of apartheid in South Africa is a clear example. One can, too, point to the earlier days of the premiership of Margaret Thatcher although, in this case, the new direction was one far less appealing for liberal democracy. Yet there does seem to be a problem with the extent to which support for political parties has become dependent on the perceived performance of their leaders alone, rather than that of the contributing whole and the ends to which they are committed. There is an issue, too, with the degree to which elected parliamentarians may lose touch with their own grass roots – either arguing against or ignoring the outcome of conference resolutions – for fear of electoral disadvantage.

This problem is exacerbated when the philosophy underpinning a political party is not clearly articulated or is in a state of flux or when those in power are at odds with one another in their understanding of it or espouse a version that differs from that of many of its supporters. Despite some very worthwhile expressions of its philosophy by political practitioners – Alan Beith and Conrad Russell are but two examples – the underpinnings of liberal democracy have never been effectively conveyed to the wider public. Support for it is, therefore, much more instinctive than grounded.

Currently, too, our own party faces a situation where what may be termed "Orange Bookery" – the belief that market forces are capable of delivering social liberal goals through a plurality of providers, allowing both a downsizing of the state and a greater empowerment of the individual – informs the thinking of a number of the more influential of our Westminster Parliamentarians, whilst many amongst its grassroots remain unconvinced. This is particularly evident here in Scotland, where the dominant ethos, across the political divides, has, arguably, tended to the "communitarian" rather than the individualist.

When Margaret Thatcher is said to have claimed that 'there is no such thing as society' she actually continued 'there is only the family'. In seeming contrast we have David Cameron saying 'There is such a thing as society. It is just different from the state'. Of course it is – but a cynic might argue that his talk of a "Big Society" amounts to no more than a recommendation that an already overburdened voluntary sector take on still more responsibility for sustaining our social goods. Yet, even so, the principle of such involvement does have a clear fit with the communitarian ethos just mentioned and the allied view of society as a family writ large – even if that family is in some respects a dysfunctional one.

Of course, it may be that there are not such great divisions between Liberal Democrats of an Orange Book persuasion and those who are not. Certainly, the contributors to the book stressed that they saw financial mechanisms as a means to the end of producing the social goods to which we would all subscribe. If so, then maybe the most serious allegation against them is that they place too great a faith in the capacity of such mechanisms to achieve the results they require. There is a good degree of evidence to show that they do not lead to an equal distribution and can rarely be rescued in terms of fairness by showing that they fit Rawls's criterion of still being to everyone's advantage.

The greatest concern, however, is that economic liberalism of this kind ceases to be seen as a means to an end and becomes an end in itself, lapsing into the kind of neo-liberalism that – at its worst – regards people simply as maximisers of their own satisfactions and determines what is valuable in life by reference to their willingness to pay for it. One might enquire as to whether the projected relaxation of planning controls in England shows a slippage in this direction.

Equally, those of a more social liberal persuasion have to guard against the accusation of stifling enterprise and encouraging dependency, of espousing protectionism, of promoting a (so-called) "Nanny State" and, even, of travelling down the route to the kind of command economy that has been rightly abandoned elsewhere. Such accusations involve a (sometimes wilful) misunderstanding of the values to which we are committed.

They do, however, force us to confront certain issues in relation to those values. How far do we see liberty as simply freedom from (mainly) legal constraints or do we need a more substantive version of what it means to be free? Surely so, if we envisage a society where "no one shall be enslaved by poverty, ignorance or conformity".

Yet, what does this mean for the values of equality and community? For example, does social liberalism embrace only equality of opportunity or does it also need to address equality of outcomes? What is our understanding of the claims and responsibilities that the individual has in relation to the community and that the community has in relation to the individual? Also, of what level of community do we speak? Can localism deliver or does it foster inequality of opportunity or outcomes or both?

In consequence, if we are to persuade others to engage with us, we must set ourselves a number of goals. First, we *have* to spell out in much more detail a basis for social liberalism in the twenty-first century and describe the kind of institutions, laws and policies appropriate to embodying this in society. Here is not the place to do so but other contributors have given strong indications of the way forward.

Second, despite the fact that liberalism is a complex philosophy, we must find a way of expressing it in ways that are readily understood. Arguably, one of the reasons for the success of the SNP is that they present people with what is a single and (apparently) simple goal – independence – and seek to reinforce the need for it at every turn. There is much to do for us in this regard. Willie Rennie's intention to link all our policy choices with the three principles of sustainability, opportunity and community is a start but only a start.

Third and finally, in doing all this we need to take nothing about the social status quo as a given. To return to the analogy of the tides, there are two interpretations of the story of King Canute. In one, he was a foolish monarch who really believed that he could turn back the waves. In another, he was a wise one who wished simply to demonstrate to fawning courtiers that there were limits even to the power of kings.

There are undoubtedly limits, too, both to the extent that it is possible to engineer social change and to what a genuinely liberal philosophy would anyway allow. But it is important to remember that many of the problems with which we have to contend are human constructs and not natural phenomena. We have to question the value of the decisions underlying them at every turn. The recent attempts to gain approval of the intended health service reforms in England, on the basis that they are simply going further down a path already taken, provide inadequate justification – if, indeed, they can be called a justification at all.

Chapter 8

Obscenities of Power and Wealth – the problem of super-high pay

Robert Brown

The banking crisis, and the revelation of the size of the pay packages enjoyed by whizz-kids in financial services, by senior executives in British industry, by top civil servants, and by media stars, has severely shaken the sense of fair play and indeed the confidence of many people in the whole economic system. What has shocked onlookers above all has been the rank greed, and the lack of any proportionality of reward or of obvious connection with merit, effort, or achievement shown by high earners, particularly in financial services and in the City.

The banking collapse brought the stark recognition that corporate greed and unaccountable power and wealth at the top could bring down the whole system and substantially damage the life chances of ordinary people who had no conceivable responsibility for the situation, nor the remotest chance of sharing even a fraction of such wealth.

The consequence was real anger and outrage, and a greater hearing for the idea that extreme gaps between the top earners and those at the bottom are seriously damaging to the overall health of society, and may go some way to explain other phenomena of the social unease and alienation which fed into drug and alcohol addiction, the irrationality of the London riots, the challenges of fractured families and fractured communities.

Researchers have increasingly realised that the unbalanced and inequitable nature of income, wealth, opportunity and reward in our increasingly unequal society is damaging to society. The point was well put by the authors of "The Spirit Level" who said that:

> *Economic growth, for so long the great engine of progress, has, in the rich countries, largely finished its work.*[6]

There are two equally obnoxious extremes. At the top, there is the obscene grossness of top executive pay – with little connection to people's economic contribution and little sense of the broader public interest; at the bottom, the damaging and illiberal emergence of what I think is correctly identified as an underclass – people and communities who have no access to opportunity or even aspiration, whose lives are blighted as children by

---

[6] The Spirit Level – Why Equality is better for Everyone – Richard Wilkinson and Kate Pickett – Penguin Books 2010 p5

disasters of parental addiction, inadequacy and poverty, and a failure of motivation, multiplied by their presence in deprived communities. This has a geographic aspect with the concentration of areas of multiple deprivation in cities like Glasgow, Liverpool and Belfast. It is claimed, for example, that Scotland would have normal European levels of mortality, morbidity, and educational achievement if Glasgow were excluded.

There is a growing recognition of the fact that this is not just an issue of poverty in a financial sense, but of a wider social malaise, a loss of individual and community values.

Someone on a low income in a society where the gap between the richest and poorest is quite narrow will have much better outcomes than someone with similar resources in a society where the gap is wide. But so will better-off people. So people in Denmark are happier, healthier and safer than people of similar means in the UK or (especially) the USA. And within the USA, relatively poor people do better in states where the gap between the poorest and the richest is least gaping.[7]

The Market and High Pay:

We view the market as the central machinery by which trade is facilitated and resources distributed, but a market constrained where necessary by civilised restraints. Most people don't go for the obscene idea that monopolistic banks or former nationalised - but still monopolistic - utilities are somehow entitled to damage

---

[7] The Spirit Level (op cit)

society and bring the economy to its knees whilst still paying executive salaries which, according to a recent report by the High Pay Commission, are 4,000 times higher than 30 years ago - 169 times more than the pay change for the average worker.[8]

Stephen Hester had no responsibility for the financial crisis but nevertheless his pay package of £7.7 million pa[9] as the current Chief Executive of the largely state-owned RBS is a moral, political and economic outrage. The publicity earlier this year focusing on his contractual bonus of nearly £1 million emphasised the lack of control which elected government felt able to exert over such matters.

The argument was that, if the Government or the Regulator intervened, then the chief executive and the Board would both walk. This nettle should certainly have been grasped at the time of the bank rescue by the then Labour Government, but no self-respecting government should accept this sort of blackmail for a minute. It is today's version of an old question – who rules in our democracy? Is it the elected government or is it a selfish oligarchy damaging to the national interest?

---

[8] ***Cheques with Balances: Why tackling high pay is in the national interest*** – Final Report of the High Pay Commission (Compass/Joseph Rowantree Social Fund) Nov 2011 p7

http://highpaycommission.co.uk/wp-content/uploads/2011/11/HPC_final_report_WEB.pdf

[9] The Guardian – 8th March 2011

Lloyds TSB is also part State owned. Its Chief Executive gets £2,572,000 pa, up by 3,141.6% over 30 years. In 1980, this was 13.6 times the wage of the average Lloyds worker; today it is 75 times that wage[10]. Average wages have gone up from £6,474 in 1980 to £25,900 today[11], up 3 times, not the 30 or 40 times increase seen in top executive pay.

Even last year, in the midst of the worst financial disaster since the Great Crash – or perhaps since the South Sea Bubble – executive pay in the FTSE-100 companies rose by an average 49% whereas ordinary workers' pay rose by just 2.7%[12].

In 1979, the top 1% took home 5.93% of the national income; by 2007, this had grown to 14.5%[13]. By 2035, it is estimated that the top 0.1% will take home 14% of the national income, a figure not seen since high Victorian Britain[14]. This sort of statistic is not seen in France, Italy, China, Japan or Sweden – only in the USA and the UK.

Claims that the national economy has increased by enormous amounts due to the efforts of these worthy top executives, who, we are told, exist in a global market place and would simply move off elsewhere if their remuneration was curbed, are risible. Further, rich

---

[10] High Pay Commission Report p23
[11] High Pay Commission Report p5
[12] Incomes Data Services (2011) Directors Pay Report.

[13] High Pay Commission Report p22

[14] High Pay Commission Report p24

people spend significant resources in trying to shape the rules of the game in their favour. .

It is curious how different arguments are used in different situations. The assertion that top people need astronomical bonuses to get them to perform (not a claim made for the rest of us) is bonkers – but it appears that this has to continue even when the entity makes a loss and where the tab is being paid by the taxpayer as it is with the key Scottish banks.

Gross inequality, as we know well in Glasgow, feeds into lower social mobility, high morbidity and mortality rates and the 20 year gap between life expectancy in Springburn and life expectancy in Bearsden.

Current Capitalism model is Bust:

But an even more significant assertion is made by the Massachusetts economist Professor Richard Wolff[15], who argues that the living standards of American workers grew for each decade of the 150 years until the 1970s. Thereafter a variety of trends - including the end of the US postwar economic hegemony, the advent of computerisation, the outsourcing of labour to other countries, and massive immigration – led to people having to work harder to pay their way, then to borrow on their homes, then to borrow on unsecured credit cards. All along, the cost of labour was flat while

---

[15] "Capitalism hits the Roof – Lecture by Prof Richard Wolff - http://www.facebook.com/l.php?u=http%3A%2F%2Fblip.tv%2Fzg raphix%2Fcapitalism-hits-the-fan-a-lecture-by-richard-wolff-on-the-economic-meltdown-5834895&h=JAQH2a0eTAQFsU0zYmLGO22bXlE3lpF5uwm9xA FK1eD2s2Q

company profits rising to astronomical levels in turn were invested in even more lending – a cycle which was unsustainable and whose bubble burst in the 2008 financial collapse. Professor Wolff argues convincingly that this is a crisis of the current model of capitalism, which cannot be remedied by short term remedies such as low interest rates, quantitative easing or a return of stricter regulation. Indeed easier borrowing will make things worse, not better.

The way forward, he claims is a growth of social enterprises and co-operatives, and the democratisation of business which should be responsible to the workforce, not the shareholders. It sounds very much like the longstanding Liberal theme of employee participation.

The challenge of Low Pay and Low Incomes:

What is the economic position of people at the bottom? We have seen that relative to top executives, low earners have not shared substantially in the proceeds of growing national wealth. It is no longer possible to contest the fact that there has been an enormous upward redistribution of income since the 1980s.

So what are we doing about it and what should we do about it?

The Coalition Government and the Financial Crisis:

Resolving the financial crisis is clearly central to this. The horrendous dilemma is that we have to retain Britain's AAA credit rating because, if we don't, the rates of Government borrowing will go up, perhaps to the 6% or 7% seen in Italy and elsewhere. This hugely increases the cost of servicing the huge debt bequeathed to us by

Gordon Brown and the bankers. On the other hand, we need economic growth because, without it, tax revenues are flat or declining, public services are squeezed and investment in infrastructure or in jobs or indeed in research and business support to grow the economy is impossible. Add to that, the crisis in the Eurozone with which we have the bulk of our trade.

Certainly, the Ratings Agencies themselves are unelected, unaccountable and often wrong – which raises other questions for Liberal Democrats – but, nevertheless, it is difficult to counter the central point here. That is the ultimate – if much belated – recognition by the markets that the values both of property assets and of financial services products were unsustainably over-valued.

Liberal Democrats can reasonably claim that our input into the Coalition Government has led to a strong Government able to avoid downgrading of our currency, and a stronger element of fairness for people across the board than would otherwise have been the case. There is also the key commitment to implement the Vickers Report on Banking and separate out normal banking from the so-called casino banking. However the implementation timetable to complete by 2019 - recommended by Vickers not the Government – seems generous and should at least have clear staging posts along the way.

Nevertheless it does not take a degree in economics to recognise that the austerity plans imposed on Ireland, Greece and Italy cannot be the last word. Ways must be found of quarantining the "toxic" debt, and allowing a return to the proper functioning of the world economy and its markets – but equally it cannot be business as usual, and the argument by Professor Wolff and others that the current model of capitalism may be bust has to be faced.

Challenges of the world economy:

For a Liberal, the structural disorders in the world economy are connected with the sheer size and unaccountability of the system as a whole and of individual entities within it, of the reduced local and even national connection that the largest companies have with communities and Governments, and of the unchecked oligarchical power they exercise.

And, in a world of finite resources, an economy whose health depends on year-by-year growth cannot sustain – it has an unhealthy and possibly fatal fever. Part of the answer may lie in a redefinition of growth to mean a growth in human happiness, in social harmony and in the scope for culture and civilisation to blossom.

The start point should be a recognition that, whilst none of us has the full answers as yet, the questions must at least include asking what is wrong with the current system and identifying that the way forward must include accepting the following propositions:

- That the current UK/US economic and social model is tending to a huge growth in the disparities between rich and poor, and that this is unjust, illiberal and damaging to society economically and socially

- That the concentrations of power and wealth in ever-larger economic entities is unnecessary, has little if any economic or social utility, and must be broken up, and offset by effective checks and balances

- That unequal societies are dysfunctional across a wide range of social outcomes

- That the fullest freedom and control over our lives and destinies requires a more human-scale economic and social organisation.

- That unlimited growth is a chimera

Fair Rewards at the Top:

The thrust of this essay is to look at how the issue of excessive top pay can be tackled.

The Coalition Government – and particularly Liberal Democrat Ministers within it – are taking some action on excess executive pay. There are moves to greater transparency by publishing fuller details of top pay packages; there is a greater focus on tackling tax avoidance by the wealthy; there is the June 2010 bank tax (increased in the 2011 Chancellor's Autumn Statement); there is Government pressure to moderate bonuses; there is talk by Vince Cable of the possibility of legislation on the subject[16].

All these are worthy short term measures, but the economic and social gains from a more equal dispensation require a radical longer term strategy:

---

[16] Reuters 14th November 2011

- **A One year period to move from bonuses to salary.**

The High Pay Commission recommended the payment of basic salaries to company executives, with remuneration committees electing to award one additional performance-related element only where it is absolutely necessary. This should be legislated on, and the change made within no more than a year.

- **End the closed shop on top remuneration.**

Remuneration at the highest levels is the province of a small cabal of powerful people who in effect decide each other's pay – a point recently made by Deputy Prime Minster Nick Clegg:

> "this closed shop of remuneration committees which seems to be too often an old boy's network …I scratch your back you scratch my back."[17]

To make matters worse, some of the key players are the pension companies and others who hold our own wealth and exercise decisions, purportedly on our behalf. But the disturbing fact is that over 40% of shares in UK publicly listed shares are in fact held by overseas investors (up from less than 4% in 1980), while the stake of long term UK investors such as pension fund and insurance companies has declined by half to under 25%[18]

---

[17] Scotsman 31st December 2011
http://www.scotsman.com/news/uk/clegg_to_tackle_top_execut ives_pay_1_1991163

[18] High Pay Commission p54

An enforceable Code of Practice should open up this network to public scrutiny, require fund managers to disclose how they vote on remuneration, and, above all, to include employee representatives on Remuneration Committees.[19]

- **End excessive high pay.**

Excessively high pay is not just a problem in financial services; the wages of the top footballers distort the economics of football; that of media personalities corrupts the BBC; Quango bosses and top civil servants are often paid by comparators with the private sector and the bonus culture has crept in there too. What was surprising about the departure of the former Metropolitan Police Commissioner Sir Paul Stephenson was not just the revelation of amazingly close police and media links, but the fact that a top civil servant thought it unexceptional – and proper - to accept "thousands of pounds' worth of free accommodation"[20] at Champneys.

There is, of course, nothing wrong with groundbreaking entrepreneurs and inventors becoming rich, nor with people being well – and proportionately - paid for success. As Nick Clegg also commented in the same speech:

"What I abhor is people who get paid bucketloads of cash in difficult times for failing."

However it should be a different ballgame for failed banks, privatised utilities, Quangos and Public Bodies. Despite the problem of legal contracts entered into for

---

[19] Recommendation of the High Pay Commission
[20] The Independent 17th July 2011

the most part by the last Government, the practice of paying bonuses to top executives in state-owned banks as a matter of routine should be ended, as should the culture of public sector bonuses.

• **Establish a Statutory High Pay Commission**

I am tempted by the suggestion in a letter to Liberal Democrat News that organisations paying more than 25 times' average wages (about £700,000) should be taxed the equivalent of the extra.[21] Perhaps more realistically, we should establish a statutory High Pay Commission to monitor high pay and pay trends, facilitate the development of pay codes (including the concept of fairness in high pay) and report annually to Government on the issue.[22]

• **Introduce a Robin Hood Tax.**

The idea of a tax on city financial transactions goes back to Keynes[23] but is more commonly referred to as a "Tobin" tax or a "Robin Hood" tax. Keynes wanted it to dampen down the unhealthy activities of speculators. Others see a tax on the buying and selling of stocks, bonds, securities, derivatives, and the other manifold activities of investment banks and hedge funds as being a way of recouping from them for the benefit of the public some of the damage done to ordinary people by the financial collapse caused by their greed.

---

[21] Letter by Humphrey Bowen – Liberal Democrat News 9th December 2011

[22] Recommendations of the High Pay Commission

[23] Keynes – General Theory on Employment, Interest and Money chap 12

There is growing support for the feasibility of such a tax[24], probably on a transnational basis (the introduction of a similar tax by Sweden alone in the late 1980s was regarded as a failure – although UK Stamp duty has existed for many years and is not dissimilar). It certainly merits a much closer look.

- **Reform of Company Law.**

There are insufficient checks and balances in company law to protect the public interest. The primary reform needed is to make companies more responsible to their employees in law and to the public interest in ethos. But we also need other changes – for example, a re-examination of the bankruptcy regime that allows companies to go bust, default on their debts and then reappear the next day as if nothing had happened. It is also not obviously in the public interest that long-established companies like Cadbury should be merged with a gigantic international conglomerate like Kraft Foods, apparently for reasons which appear anti-competitive; nor indeed that companies should be acquired in ways which leave a huge millstone of debt around their necks – a phenomenon, affecting, for example, some football clubs. These are complex area but ones we ignore at our peril.

---

[24] Notably by Lord Turner, Chairman of the Financial Services Authority – The Guardian – 27th August 2009 http://www.guardian.co.uk/business/2009/aug/27/fsa-bonus-city-banks-tax

One example worth examination is the set up of the Edrington Group, a large whisky company headquartered in Glasgow which is 100% owned by the Robertson Trust. This arrangement affects the company ethos for the better but also protects it against takeover.

There remains the issue of whether radical moves against excessive executive pay, and not least a Robin Hood tax would be damaging to the UK economy and to the financial services sector in particular. This is not a negligible issue but we should regard with extreme scepticism much of the special pleading that comes from the sector.

It is worth observing that the House of Commons Public Accounts Committee recently came to the view that major firms were allowed off with more than £25 billion in "unresolved tax bills" as a result of deals with HM Revenue & Customs.[25]

Tackling the excesses of high pay cannot be looked at in isolation. It is linked with creating a justified sense of fairness across the board, with reducing the worst extremities of power and wealth. It is part of a wider need to reform and rebalance a form of capitalism which has become cancerous, damages the public interest and destroys the lives of ordinary people.

Already the arrogance of top executives is back, the arguments are being marshalled, fears raised, obstacles

---

[25] Reported BBC News 20th December 2011 -
    http://www.bbc.co.uk/news/business-16253205

created. It is not too much to say that success in getting on top of this issue will determine the whole shape of our society for years to come – as will failure. It is a battle which Liberal Democrats must lead with vigour. Three fully equipped Bank Chief Executives costs as much to keep as the scrapped Nimrod warplanes – but Chief Executives are just as great a terror, and they last longer![26]

---

[26] Adapted from Lloyd George's Newcastle speech on the House of Lords - "A fully equipped Duke costs as much to keep up as two Dreadnoughts, and Dukes are just as great a terror, and they last longer." 9 October 1909, printed in the *Manchester Guardian* on October 11, 1909.

Chapter 9

Public Services for the 21st Century

Nigel Lindsay

What do we need from public services in the future, and why? If we do need them, how are we to pay for them as we emerge from recession? Why should government, either at national or local level, be responsible for services that could be delivered by the private sector or voluntary organizations? This paper aims to set out the Liberal principles that underpin high-quality public services, to learn from international evidence of the value of maintaining such services, to propose that there is inherent value in local provision and accountability, and to reaffirm the need for the provision of effective public services to be a high priority in the spending plans of any Liberal or Liberal-influenced government

For Liberals, the purpose of government is to create the optimum conditions for each individual to realise his or her potential. That means ensuring that individuals have the freedom to decide how best to live their lives, while removing the hindrances to their so doing. The influential Liberal philosopher Thomas Hill Green set out principles that are strikingly modern today. TH Green wrote that the state should foster the social, political and economic environments in which individuals can have the best chance of acting according to their consciences. Green developed his academic philosophy into practical involvement in the municipal life of Oxford and its Liberal Association, and understood the reality of life for those born with fewer advantages. He stressed that individuals are only free to make meaningful choices when the inequities that circumscribe the choices available to them are mitigated. In our age, this implies that governments should ensure the provision of good quality public services such as education, public transport, health and social care.

Green was writing in the nineteenth century and his thinking had a practical effect on Liberals in government from the premiership of Campbell-Bannerman onwards. Campbell-Bannerman, his Ministers, and later Liberals such as Beveridge put in place the main principles of the welfare state which underpin so many of the improvements in the UK's standard of living over the past 60 years. In contrast, a central weakness of conservatism is its willingness to embrace the principles of free individual choice while turning a blind eye to the constraints which severely limit the number of people actually free to make a particular choice – the shallow concept of freedom satirised as "the freedom to dine at The Ritz".

Ideas similar to Green's were brought into the public eye in the autumn of 2011 as a consequence of protestors occupying the City of London. This occupation led indirectly to the resignation of the chancellor of St Paul's Cathedral, Giles Fraser. Quoted in *The independent* after his resignation, he was critical of the current Prime Minister's call for a return to morality. Canon Fraser insisted that morality should be applied to society as well as to the individual and said:

> *David Cameron seems to define morality in terms of the individual but there is a common morality and I don't think he gets that aspect of morality. He doesn't get there are steep structural problems we need to answer."*

Those structural problems for me concern whether or not everyone in the UK feels they have the same opportunity for self-realisation. Unfortunately it is clear that millions of people in this country have very little chance to realise their own potential. Sometimes this is due to lack of an adequate education, sometimes it stems from ill-health or poor housing, sometimes from enslavement to drug or alcohol addiction and of course often from many other obstacles which can be mitigated by services provided by local or national government.

Wilkinson and Pickett point out in their acclaimed 2009 book *The Spirit Level*, that a high level of government services is not necessary in countries such as Japan where a relatively high degree of equality exists between the market incomes (earnings before tax and benefits) of high and low earners. By contrast, some redistribution in the form of services paid for by taxation is necessary in countries such as the UK where (as Robert Brown points out elsewhere in this booklet) the share of national income appropriated by the UK's highest earners has increased exponentially over the past three decades. For as long as gross income inequality persists in the UK, it must be the responsibility of government and its agencies to minimise the obstacles to self-realisation that result, and to provide the conditions for "positive liberty" – that is, the circumstances in which each citizen has meaningful equality of opportunity to live their lives in the best way possible.

The evidence from elsewhere

The former Taoiseach Garret FitzGerald, a good friend of Liberalism, is reported once to have interrupted a colleague's explanation of how a policy would work by saying "Yes, yes, I see how it would work in practice. But how would it work in theory?" This may be a myth, but it is right for Liberals to develop theories of government and service provision from their core principles. Once formed, though, such theories need to be assessed for workability and practical effect. A good way of doing this, and a method true to the Liberal tradition, is by international perspectives. Such comparisons can be seen to support the approach outlined in this essay.

This paper started by setting out a purpose of government which for Liberals is to create the optimum conditions for each individual to realise his or her potential. Success in this is to some extent a subjective matter and therefore difficult to measure accurately. Useful tools have been developed in recent decades, among which is the OECD Life Satisfaction survey. This survey measures how people evaluate their life as a whole, rather than their current feelings. It aims to capture a reflective assessment of the life circumstances and conditions that are important for subjective wellbeing.   Denmark, Canada, Norway and The Netherlands rank highest in the latest survey, and four of the Nordic countries figure in the top ten places. In contrast, the UK ranks fifteenth out of thirty-four.

Nordic countries as a group achieve strikingly good results from their public services. They enjoy both a long-standing social democratic culture of being prepared to pay for good services and a lack of the glaring income inequalities we experience in Scotland and the UK. They also have local government devolved to the most local level. These factors help the Nordic countries produce better outcomes in crime limitation, literacy, mental and physical health, lower rates of teenage pregnancy and obesity and many other measures. After noting this, the authors of *The Spirit Level* conclude that "Inequality seems to make countries socially dysfunctional across a wide range of outcomes". This supports the proposal that increasing inequality in the UK needs to be corrected by provision of effective public services financed by redistributive taxation.

Finland provides interesting evidence in the field of education. Finnish school-leavers have among the highest rates of literacy and numeracy achieved anywhere in the world. Their rates are certainly far ahead of those achieved in Scotland – 98% as against 80%. Yet these results are attained with lower inputs than in Scotland, and over a shorter school career. Among the factors helping Finns to this achievement are freedom to decide on teaching methods at the most local level, and a strong network of public libraries

Interestingly, four Nordic countries are listed among the ten least corrupt in the world, according to Transparency International's 2010 Corruption Perceptions Index. New Zealand, Australia and Canada are also among the ten least corrupt. Shamefully, the UK has fallen to 16th place, and it was reported in January this year that KPMG's Fraud Barometer recorded a rise of 150% to a record £3.5bn in alleged fraud in the UK during 2011, much of it apparently by companies' own management. It should be obvious that the countries perceived as least corrupt are those whose success we have good cause to envy. There is a strong case for establishing rigorous standards of reputable public and personal ethics, as well as open-ness and transparency in light of this. Certainly recent revelations about the National Audit Office, HMRC, the Metropolitan Police and others suggests that the distinction between public service and private benefit is not taken as seriously now as it should be by some very senior public servants. That trend, if not arrested, leads directly to difficulties which have become obvious in some Mediterranean countries.

Do we need alternative means of delivery?

To establish the need for government and its agencies to ensure a high level of provision of public services is obviously not to say that the present level is correct and that the means of service delivery used are the best that can be imagined. Woeful tales of gross shortcomings in local authority social services, and national services such as the police and health service have become all too common. It would be wrong not to accept that these shortcomings, whether they result from isolated instances of mismanagement or from corporate cultures, show a need to review how services can be best provided on an efficient basis that meets the needs of service users. On occasion, public service providers have seemed to stultify and become self-sustaining, guarding provider interests at the expense of consumers. There are of course honourable exceptions to this trend, public bodies that develop and innovate in their delivery of services. Such good practice needs to be universalised more effectively.

Nor can the private sector claim to be superior in delivering services where they have taken on responsibility. The 1980s mantra that it does not matter who owns the mechanism for service delivery so long as the service is delivered was always suspect. As Ben Colburn points out in his essay, there is at least an element of public accountability, however tortuous, when services are delivered by elected bodies. That accountability is removed if private companies deliver services. Instead, private companies are accountable to shareholders and creditors. That these can have a baleful influence will have been painfully obvious to those who were meant to have been cared for by businesses that have recently been in the news. These include Southern Cross whose care homes closed abruptly in 2011, Castlebeck, which claimed to be unaware of the completely unacceptable behaviour of staff at a care home for which it had responsibility, and the private clinics which profited from breast implants but refused to pay to put matters right when these were found to be sub-standard. Private monopolies, it seems, are even worse than public monopolies.

Devolving services to the third sector has some attractions and some voluntary sector organisations have provided very high quality and responsive services. Examples include the Prince's Trust, the hospice movement and the Glasgow Old Peoples' Welfare Association. However such services rarely take over the whole of the service provision in their field or area. There may be ways in which this could be developed into a viable model but it is probably more satisfactory when the Third Sector provides a complementary service rather than attempting to replicate the role of the Council or Health Board. Further, despite its greater flexibility, the sector can suffer from the same lack of accountability as the private sector and perhaps inevitably carries even greater financial risks. The third sector and co-ops can also fall prey to a type of corporate ambition in which the winning and retention of contracts for service delivery becomes fundamental to their economic security and starts to take precedence over their core aims. In such circumstances, understandable as they are, co-ops and voluntary organizations lose the distinctiveness that made them attractive at the start and become less and less distinct from private companies.

Empowering people and their communities

Localism – the policy that services are best delivered by the authority closest to those who use them, and whose members are most readily accountable to the electorate - has always been a cornerstone of Liberal belief. It lies behind our insistence that the police and other emergency services in Scotland should continue to be run at regional level rather than centrally. It applies with equal force to the delivery of, and accountability for, other services such as health and social services, education, road and rail services, libraries, refuse collection and so forth.

However, for Liberals, localism has another component – which is the right of local communities below Council level to be empowered to identify their own needs and run some of their own services in appropriate ways.

Indeed, it is worth noting here that Scotland has a long way to go before it can lay claim to truly local government, and that many other European countries manage their affairs effectively on a level much closer to the grass roots. Local government in Finland, for instance, is delivered very successfully by over 400 councils while Scotland with a similar population has only 32, many of which struggle. This leads to councils here being perceived as more remote, and there is far less chance of people knowing their Councillor personally or of living close by them. Council sizes in Scotland are much larger than the European average, and this means that they frequently can't achieve the "buy-in" that would help them operate more effectively and it is harder for the people they claim to serve, to hold them to account. In contrast every village in France has its own Mairie and local government structure, offering a prospect of involvement in decision-making in a way we have not seen in Scotland since we relinquished our parish councils in 1929.

Paddy Ashdown has made the point forcefully that more localised decision-making will inevitably lead to different standards of service delivery in different areas.

Liberals accept this and should not complain of "postcode lotteries", as John Aldridge points out, so long as genuine accountability is in place to ensure that the differing levels of provision authentically reflect differing levels of demand. That is certainly preferable to the "one size fits all" approach which has characterised the Labour Party's approach practically since its inception. Local decision-making, though, must also mean strong local lines of accountability – without this, localism is a debased concept.

Local delivery of services depends on the competence of the people who run them. There have been well-publicised instances where a small local authority or health authority has been seen to be incompetent, and whose service has been taken over by a neighbouring but larger authority. Better management follows, though the economies of scale claimed for such mergers are questionable, as John Seddon's work suggests. If we are to deliver services at the most local level, we need to rely on more than the goodwill of those elected and sadly, there is frequently a lack of good leadership in the most vulnerable of communities. So how can communities develop competent leadership? The best approach I know consists of programmes to build the capacity of communities and develop leadership talents within them.

A successful capacity-building approach will involve a number of agencies. Voluntary groups, library and other resource services, CABx, welfare rights and consumer agencies and perhaps the post office network can all play a part in disseminating information and providing opportunities to identify and develop the expertise and leadership skills that can help a community in its development. Such work will require adequate public funding and will need to be long-term rather than one-off. The prizes for capacity-building will be worthwhile. Chief among them will be an increase in the ability of willing communities to take greater charge of their own affairs, to assess their own needs, and to provide and monitor services accordingly. Such an outcome would be true "people power", and as different as chalk from cheese both from the collectivism advocated by some thinkers within the Labour Party, and from the woolliness of the "big society" proposed but not defined by the Prime Minister and some conservative theorists.

Paying for public services

Good public services are costly. For too long there has been pressure to reduce the cost to the government of providing services, and this has unfortunately taken precedence over what seems to me the more important priority of ensuring that we have a healthy, well-educated population, free from the barriers to self-development which presently constrain the contribution each can make to the common good. It is often claimed that we no longer have the resources to pay for good public services, but this is in reality just a way of saying the speaker no longer wishes to give priority to such spending. There has been no shortage of cash to pay for illegal wars and oil-related military expeditions to other continents, for instance. Public services need to be restored to high priority in the government's spending plans.

As a student slogan said "If you think education is expensive, try ignorance!" The same principle applies in many other areas. If all the population of working age were well-educated, healthy and motivated, the economy would improve dramatically and the so-called pensions crisis would largely evaporate. Yet there is reluctance to pay for this among those most able to do so. The very entrepreneurs and business organisations (often closely linked to the Conservative Party) who whinge about school-leavers who can't read or write satisfactorily are often the same ones who complain most loudly about the prospect of increased taxation that could remedy the situation.

Labour governments under Blair and Brown sought to evade full responsibility for the provision of high-quality public services by promoting the Public Finance Initiative and its successors. These schemes, little more than a ruse to move spending off the government's accounts, involved high costs, lack of accountability, and shifting payment for current consumption on to future generations. The coalition government has not ended these, nor has the SNP government in Scotland. In each case, public service spending has been compromised by pressure for further cuts and privatisations.

There is another way. That is to recognise that it is in the interests of everyone and of every corporation to have and to pay for safe roads, efficient railways, good education, crime-free streets, lower rates of avoidable illness, effective public health measures and clean environments. News International and its directors need, and should pay generously towards, the road network which distributes its products and the education system that supplies its recruits. Vodafone and its directors need and should pay willingly towards the safe and healthy environment that enables its customers to buy and use its products. Banks should recognize that the overpaid work of their traders and executives would be useless if a lack of efficient sanitation caused their offices to be over-run with disease and so it is in their interest and that of their employees to contribute fully to the costs of public health provision. Yet during 2011 a sorry tale has unraveled of such vast corporations seeking to minimise their contributions to the common good, and HMRC – unbelievably – settling with them for amounts that seem much smaller than might have been achieved.

The need for companies to pay their share of tax willingly carries an obvious corollary for individuals, and we must accept that imposing higher levels of taxation than those we have grown used to may be unpopular, though perhaps not as unpopular as is commonly asserted. The latest (2010) *British Social Attitudes* survey suggests that the percentage of people who support higher taxation to enable higher spending on education, healthcare and social security rises during boom years but falls during recessions. Yet even now, near the trough of a recession, the survey reports that 40% of Scots say they are prepared to pay higher taxes to finance more spending in these areas. Ten years ago, the figure was around 60% and it will probably rise to that level again as the recession eases. We need to win the argument that taxation spent on social goods such as health, education and social care will ultimately save costs. There is nothing unjust about this, nor is it a new idea. The Labour Party nowadays shrinks from facing even the need to discuss this question. It is for Liberals, who can be sure most of their voters support redistributive taxation, to explain why it is necessary and to provide the focus for those who agree.

International experience teaches us that people are more willing to accept high rates of tax for the common good when they are confident that others are not avoiding their share. We know also that higher taxation is more likely to be accepted when the results are obvious, and when officialdom is seen as helpful and enabling, rather than self-serving or corrupt. This in turn can be achieved more easily when government exists in small-scale units and is both closer and more immediately accountable to the people it serves.

Leading the debate

We have seen that inequality on the scale that has developed in Scotland and the UK over the last three decades is harmful to the whole of our society and everyone who lives in it. There are countries not very far from us and of similar size, which out-perform us on many measures that affect individual happiness and welfare. The best way to correct the wide gap in life chances that results from unreasonably large variances in income is the provision by government of effective public services, run in an ethical context and financed in proportion to their earnings by citizens and companies through tax.

It is for Liberals to lead the way in arguing this case as no other party can be relied upon to so do. We made the same case and won over the electorate to lay the foundations of the welfare state in the early 20th century. We made it again in the middle of the century to enable the foundation of the NHS and a universal system of social security. We need to make it even more forcefully now to ensure that post-recession Scotland has the effective public services that are needed to make it a healthy, functional, and just society.

We need also to recognize that how we deliver public services influences the quality of those services and the potential for users to hold providers satisfactorily to account. That necessitates local delivery, and informed, well-led communities

TH Green's view of the state as ensuring that individuals have the freedom to decide how best to live their lives, while removing the hindrances to their so doing, remains as accurate a summary of the Liberal position as ever. His assertion that individuals are only free to make meaningful choices when the inequities that circumscribe the choices available to them are mitigated, resonates with Scotland in 2012 where inequalities remain very much in evidence and need to be reduced by common purpose. Liberal Democrats need to address this and develop proposals for specific actions in response. That will require detailed debate, for which I hope this paper provides some pointers.

Chapter 10

Paying for the big outlays – degrees, homes and old age

Ross Finnie

Introduction

Who should pay for studying for a degree or the provision of social housing or care for the elderly? Should it be the state, the private individual or perhaps through means testing or a combination of both? These questions are being asked in the context of the economic collapse of 2008 that has necessitated substantial reductions in public expenditure and the fact that the Conservative/Liberal Democrat Coalition Government has introduced measures in England to: replace 80 per cent. of university funding with student fees and require graduates earning above a fixed threshold to repay their fees; and increase the involvement of the private sector in the NHS. The question, in principle, of who pays engages some basic tenets of Liberal philosophy that go wider than the provision of university education, housing and care of the elderly and encompasses all benefits provided by the welfare state

The Classic liberals of the eighteenth and early nineteenth centuries although championing individual liberties, never saw the need for the intervention of the state. Hobson and Hobhouse changed Liberal thinking to accept the need for a leading role for government in order to achieve social and economic progress. This change of direction was built upon by Keynes and Beveridge actively promoting the welfare state that developed in the post-war period. One of the leading theorists of classical liberalism of the twentieth century, Hayek, warned, however, in *The Road to Serfdom*, that the interventionist welfare-providing state thus created would grow too powerful and endanger personal freedom.

In recent times, despite concerns about individual decision making and choice, there had been little debate within the Liberal Democrat Party about either the need or scope of the state in welfare provision - until the publication of *The Orange Book* in 2004 which strongly criticised what it calls Fabian welfare as having led to a pattern of dependency and looked for a return to a more economic (Classic) liberal model.

The ensuing debate within the Party has confirmed health and education as classic public goods that should remain free at the point of use. The issue of choice in public services remains problematic and centres on two fundamental issues. One is the scope for, and limits of, personal choice within a public service without subverting the public nature of the service. The other is to define the best mechanisms for exercising choice in public services. This might be achieved by supplementing core public services with private provision or using vouchers or social insurance mechanisms to simulate markets, or simply trying to create more variety within the public services.

It is against that background that this chapter examines the question of who should pay for the provision of university education, social housing and care of the elderly.

University Degrees

Over the past decade or so the debate about who should pay for University fees has been fuelled far more by concerns about cost than any other political or philosophical consideration. Incredibly, despite mounting costs, there has been no fundamental debate as to whether the purpose and structure of degree courses and their method of delivery are fit for purpose.

In 1996 the Conservative government commissioned the Dearing Report into the funding of higher education. The Labour Government was in power by the time the Report was published and it accepted the main thrust of the Report. In 1988, it introduced means tested (family income threshold £23,000) student fees of £1,000 per annum. The maximum level of fee was subsequently increased to £3,000 in 2004.

Scottish Liberal Democrats fought the first Scottish Parliament election in 1999 with a commitment to abolish student fees. In the coalition negotiations with the Scottish Labour Party that followed, there was a total impasse on the issue of student fees and the matter was remitted to an Independent Committee of Inquiry into Student Finance under Andrew Cubie.

The Cubie Report formed the basis of a compromise within the Coalition whereby: tuition fees for further education would be paid for by the state; tuition fees for full-time undergraduate courses would be abolished; access bursaries for poorer students would be re-introduced; and a Graduate Endowment Scheme would be established under which graduates would contribute a maximum of £2,000 payable under the student loan scheme mechanism which had an income threshold of £10,000. In 2007, the minority SNP Government brought forward a Bill to abolish the Graduate Endowment which was passed with the support of the Scottish Liberal Democrats

In 2009 the Labour Government at Westminster established the Browne Review into the Future of Higher Education Funding which reported in October 2010. The Conservative/Liberal Democrat Coalition Government accepted the principal findings of the Browne Review and, with a number of important changes, introduced a system for England that reduced the universities' teaching grant by 80 per cent replacing it with tuition fees, the cap on which was increased from £3,000 to £9,000, provided student loans to avoid any up-front payment of fees and required graduates to repay their loans by means of a 9 per cent surcharge on their future earnings over a threshold of £21,000. This it was claimed would put University funding on a sustainable basis and provide for a fair means for graduates who could afford it to repay their fees.

Liberals have long believed that education is a classic public good. The state has a legitimate concern to ensure that its people have access to a level of education and or training that not only enables the individual to develop his/her talents but also enables a person to serve the community, engage in all forms of research or enter the industrial or commercial labour market. Investing to produce the educated capital of a nation is probably the most important investment a state can make. For Liberals that investment must provide equality of access, a fair choice and an appropriate level of quality.

If all individuals are to have equal access, it follows that education and training, at all levels, should be free at the point of delivery. Whilst there is evidence that increasing student fees, even where equivalent levels of grant or bursary funding is made available, has a negative effect on student up-take, the evidence from Scotland indicates that making university education free at the point of delivery does not guarantee equal access. Over the past five years, during which there have been no up-front fees, the average rate of participation of lower socio-economic groups has remained stubbornly low at 26-28 per cent compared to 45-47 per cent for Scotland as a whole.

Liberals want the individual to be able to exercise choice: over the type of course; which university to attend; and to have some influence over the quality of the educational experience. As pointed out in the introductory paragraphs, however, providing real choice in a state provided service is not easy. In general terms the Scottish Funding Council (SFC) allocates funding largely on the basis of historical activity but it also takes account of other factors such as the geographical provision of courses and the range of course provision. Application of the SFC's formula is intended to ensure an appropriate range of courses and universities from which the student can exercise choice.

In England, the Government no longer funds universities directly but does so through the student. Student choice and the market it creates determines the funding of the university. Whether that system widens student choice in real terms, however, depends on the extent to which the Government exercises control over public expenditure by capping student numbers. If it does, as in Scotland, then there is a real limitation on the ability of funding through students to have a material effect on student choice.

Liberals also care about quality and the individual student's ability to influence quality. The SFC sets quality standards but in the main it adopts the Government's agenda. Whilst many of the standards will benefit students it does not provide students with a role in standard setting, One of the reasons given for allowing funding to follow the student was to give universities an incentive to improve teaching. As the distribution mechanisms already take account of student numbers, however, it is difficult to see why switching from a grant distribution method to a student fee method will produce any material improvement in quality.

Both Cubie in Scotland and Browne in England concluded that as university graduates on average go on to earn substantially more than those entering the labour market from other forms of training it was right that they should contribute to the cost of their university education, Taking the English example if the graduate earns above £21,000 then the graduate starts to make a contribution and this is said to be fair because a graduate on these earnings can afford it.

Liberals have cause to be concerned with the Cubie and Browne conclusions on three grounds. First, if the argument is that any individual who can afford it should repay the cost of their higher education then, apart from discriminating against graduates, this is simply a contingent form of means testing which is at odds with the free provision of classic public goods.

Second, whilst the English proposal is not a tax, largely to avoid the graduate paying more than the cost of his/her fees and loans, the fact remains that, whilst repaying the fees, the effect on the individual is the same as an increase in his/her marginal rate of tax. A progressive form of income tax is fair because, without exception, all taxpayers earning the most pay the most. Effectively introducing an additional rate band because of how you were trained or educated does not make progressive taxation fairer.

Third, given that one of the Liberal objectives of the exercise is to remove financial barriers to the individual developing his/her talents to the fullest, it seems a perverse incentive to succeed if the price of that success is to crystallise a contingent liability to repay the cost of your training.

In January 2012 the Scottish Government announced a package of £1.02 billion - an average increase of some 14 per cent to universities - to match the level of funding available to English universities. It came with strings, including more central control which is inimical to Liberal thinking. That sum, however, is the cost to the state of funding university education and difficult choices will have to be made elsewhere in the budget. That leaves the question of whether that cost can be controlled and/or reduced by switching funding to student fees. Economic commentators reviewing the graduate repayment scheme have queried some of the assumptions, particularly now that over 65 per cent of universities are to charge fees of £9,000. The majority of commentators agree that, in cash terms, the proposals will increase public expenditure through this Parliament and into the next. Beyond that, whilst there is no unanimity amongst commentators, none is forecasting a significant saving to the public purse. In the absence of a compelling financial argument, Liberals should continue to support state funded university education.

Homes

Social changes have led to a fall in the size of the average household and, consequently, a rise in demand for housing. In addition, demographic change, particularly an aging population, has meant that more houses are needed for older people and for those with special care needs. The existence of a well established private housing sector has meant that, in recent years, the state has confined its interventions in the housing sector largely to assisting those on lower incomes by way of housing benefit, tackling homelessness, and supporting the provision of affordable housing. The term "affordable housing" originally referred to socially rented housing but has been extended to include intermediate rented accommodation and subsidised owner-occupied housing.

Liberals do not regard housing as a classic public good to be provided free at the point of delivery. The interventions, summarised above, have been supported and in some cases promoted by Liberals because they mirrored Liberal values about the individual's right to housing of a decent standard and the ability of the individual to exercise choice particularly where special needs are an issue.

Despite huge investment in housing over many years by governments of different political persuasion there are still major problems to be resolved. In Scotland in 2010-11: 62 per cent of social housing was below the Scottish Housing Quality Standard; 298,000 homes were affected by dampness or condensation; 44 per cent failed the energy standard - our homes emit twice as much CO_2 as our cars; and 41,550 households were accepted by their local authority as homeless or potentially homeless despite the provisions of the Homelessness (Scotland) Act 2003 which set the target of ending homelessness by the end of 2012.

The Scottish Government cut the housing and regeneration budget from £448 million to £391 million for 2011-2012. Without arguing about the precise sum, Liberal values would support public spending at these levels in order to: eliminate homelessness; pay for the supply of new affordable housing to ensure good quality housing for the large number of households who do not have the means to afford satisfactory housing; provide appropriate housing for disabled people; and invest in energy efficiency.

Individual choice needs to be protected. There are clearly economies of scale to be achieved through harnessing the collective purchasing power of local authorities and housing associations but that cannot be at the expense of diminishing the power of the local authority or housing association. There is also a case for examining the balances built up by housing associations properly to maintain the condition of their assets to ensure that there are no surpluses that could be better deployed. The biggest impediment to the sustainable development of the housing sector in general and the socially rented sector in particular is the availability and price of land.

The unsustainable housing boom that preceded the financial crash of 2008 which was largely fuelled by the ready availability of credit pushed up land values as demand increased which in turn drove up prices and encouraged speculative purchases and sales. The increase in land values impacted severely on the ability of the socially rented sector to expand. The boom has now been replaced with a "housing crisis" Cheap credit has gone, mortgages require to be supported by substantial deposits, there is no incentive to bring Scotland's 70,000 empty properties back into occupation and landowners are waiting for an up-turn in the market before releasing land for new housing. In the provision of social housing the chronic shortage of affordable housing continues.

Liberals, with their long-term commitment to sustainable development, have to be concerned that only four years after the financial and housing collapse there are already fears being expressed that house prices aren't rising quickly enough and banks are being criticised for being too restrictive with mortgages. The seeds of another unsustainable property boom are being sown. Until the earlier part of the twentieth century Liberals advocated Land Value Taxation (LVT) to provide, amongst other reasons, a fiscal framework that militated against land value speculation. In the present circumstances and taking a long-term view about containing land values and thus the cost of social housing there is a case for arguing that LVT's time has come.

Introducing LVT as a replacement for council tax and non-domestic rates would have the following benefits. It would act as a disincentive to speculative activities aimed at increasing land values because the increase would be taxed under LVT. It would also act as a disincentive to holding on to vacant or derelict land, including land with planning permission, or land with vacant properties because whilst at present there is little or no cost in so doing LVT would be levied on the undeveloped value of the land. Clearly there can be no guarantees, market forces will prevail but LVT would have the Liberal virtue of acting to stabilise land values which would be for the benefit of both the public and private housing sectors.

Old age

Since the publication of William Beveridge's seminal report in 1942 Liberals have supported the concept of a national health service free at the point of delivery. Interestingly, in the context of people living longer but not necessarily in good health, one of Beveridge's early descriptions of his proposals was - the prevention and comprehensive treatment of ill health. Liberals have continued to regard the provision of health care as a classic public good to be financed by progressive taxation although certain elements of the NHS provision, notably dentistry and optometry, are now more often provided on a private basis.

Scottish Liberal Democrats helped to introduce Free Personal and Nursing Care (FPNC) for the elderly in 2002. The cost in 2003-04 amounted to £219 million and by 2009-10 it had nearly doubled to £426 million This dramatic rise in cost is largely attributable to: a 12 per cent increase in the number of self funders in care homes; a 41 per cent increase in the number receiving free personal care at home; and the proportion of local council older home care clients increasing from 57 per cent to 86 per cent. The increases in costs have provoked a continuing debate about whether the policy is affordable.

FPNC, however, should not be seen in isolation but rather it should be considered in the totality of care for the elderly. The Scottish Government estimates that the total health and social care costs for some 90,000 people aged over 65 was around £4.5 billion in 2006-07. The numbers aged over 65 are expected to increase by 21 per cent by 2016 and by 144 per cent by 2031. The Scottish Government estimates that if the same level of service is provided in the same way then the costs will increase to reflect the demographic changes from the £4.5 billion to £5.6 billion by 2016 and to £8 billion by 2031.

These projected levels of expenditure pose real challenges to the way in which the current system is delivered, the way in which it is funded and its free provision at the point of delivery. The current system is delivered by the NHS, local councils, the private sector and the voluntary sector. To try and coordinate the delivery of care in the community including care for the elderly, at the instigation of the Scottish government, Community Health Partnerships and Community Health and Care Partnerships (CH(C)Ps) were set up by the Health Boards and local councils across Scotland. Liberals supported the concept of CH(C)Ps believing that they offered an opportunity not only to coordinate community care better but also for Health Boards and local councils to devolve the delivery of local care to local communities.

The performance of CH(C)Ps across Scotland has been mixed but across the piece they have not really fulfilled their objectives and they have failed to meet the Liberal aim of devolving more power to local communities. In addition a number of studies have shown that better delivery could be effected and considerable financial savings could be made if the original concept could be put into effect.

The Liberal drivers in the care of the elderly include the imperative of: treating the elderly person as an individual; respecting the wish to retain the maximum degree of independence for as long as possible; acknowledging the preference to stay at home; and providing for individual care needs, To deliver on these drivers a Liberal care model for the elderly would have the following characteristics. It would not only want people to live longer but to be healthy for longer and that would mean putting more emphasis on anticipatory and preventative approaches to care. It would involve a shift in the balance of care, moving from residential settings and hospitals to people's own homes. It would harness modern technology in the form of telecare, telemedicine and e-health. It would offer a range of self-directed support to tailor care to individual needs. The delivery mechanism would be decentralised in a community based integrating health and social care service, underpinned by a care model that ensures equality of standards across the country.

A Liberal care model for the elderly could therefore not only satisfy better the needs of the individual it could also realise the financial savings experts have suggested are there to be made. The cost of care for the elderly will still be considerable and if it is not to be met by the state do we have to consider some form of means testing? People fear the loss of their independence generally, the loss of dignity and becoming financially dependent on someone else in their old age. Means testing does nothing to allay such fears; indeed it exacerbates them. Little wonder then that the Sutherland Report which recommended FPNC said that the cost of personal care of the elderly reflected the true risk and catastrophic nature of needing long-term care and concluded that it was right for the state to exempt personal care from means testing altogether.

Part of the problem of funding the cost of old age is the generally inadequate level of the state funded old age pension which arises from it being funded by National Insurance contributions on a pay-as-you-go basis. This means for example in the year 2010-11, for the UK as a whole, the National Insurance Fund paid out total benefits of some £74 bullion (£69 billion on old age pensions) which was slightly in excess of the National Insurance contributions received and ended with a balance of some £6 billion. One of the consequences of this short-term method of funding is that if old age pensions are not up-rated in line with the cost of living not only is the rate of pension payable insufficient to meet the cost of elderly care there is no ready source to help fill the gap.

Beveridge's original idea was that, over time, his proposed National Insurance Scheme should become fully-funded. His final Report was modified to take account of Treasury concerns about cost. One of the modifications came as a result of Maynard Keynes advising Beveridge to fund pensions not out of an accumulated fund but out of current income. Keynes argued that it would be a severe burden to meet simultaneously the cost of pensions against which no funds had been accumulated and to accumulate funds for future pensions. He suggested that the future can well be left to look after itself.

In the financial climate at the end of the second-world war that might have been sage advice. It has, however, had serious long-term consequences by leaving the adequacy of old age pension provision to the vagaries of the economic decisions of the government of the day. Four years after the worst financial crisis in living memory is probably not the most propitious time to suggest that Beveridge's original proposals on funding should be revisited. However, individuals are going to continue to live longer and, even with better preventative care making them healthier for longer, proper and adequately financed care of the elderly will remain a major long-term problem.

For Liberals pursuing a more sustainable agenda, a long-term solution to the long-term problem of care for the elderly has to be high on the agenda. A fully funded National Insurance scheme will not solve the problem. A progressive move towards such a position, however, would open up the possibility of not only being able to meet these long-term care costs but also to examine critically just what precisely the state intends the old age pension to provide for.

Chapter 11

Private and Public Sector – Costs, Monopoly and Accountability

Paul Coleshill

At the end of the Soviet Union Neo-Con advisors suggested removing all controls over "free" markets. The Russian Mafia reached for their guns, they knew that the really "free" way to get assets was to shoot and take. The very least markets require is enforceable individual property rights and contracts. This in turn requires the coercive force of law - always sanctioned, and usually provided - by the state.

Liberal Democrats understand that markets are not directly ordained by God, they are made by people as a set of social constraints, and that, when markets work through voluntary exchange, they tend to make everyone better off.

The problem is that when the cost of contract construction monitoring and enforcement are very high for one or both parties to an exchange, or there is no freedom to choose, for example because of monopoly or dire need, markets fail - they don't enable 'free' exchange. The reality is that few real world market transactions consist of two equally powerful and well informed individuals, freely exchanging well understood assets to mutual advantage

Since Liberals believe in the worth of constrained individual property rights (as motivating individual effort) and law (as a route to justice) we all advocate the construction of at least the minimum social constraints that enable markets.

What not all Liberal Democrats have appreciated in recent years is that there are huge public costs in maintaining markets. Claiming that the private sector provides the "wealth" that the public sector relies on - and pleading "don't kill the goose" by regulation or taxation, leads to the absurdity of regarding investment in the Post Office telephone system as a luxury provided at private sector expense but investment in British Telecom (plc) investment (in exactly the same exchanges) as good for the economy. This way lies the madness of PFI.

The private sector is not unique in providing resources to maintain the "luxury" of the public sector; the public sector provides resources to maintain the private sector. Transferring; hospitals, the police force, all education and roads, all water and railways, all electrical and gas supply to the private sector does not do away with the (private sector) demand for them; they still need to be paid for - just not from tax.

What is the nature and extent of the social intervention needed to sustain markets and/or replace them? Should we advocate a bit of market failure (supermarket giants?); or regulate (telephone common carrier enforcement?); or provide directly through a state agent (the NHS?). Individual empowerment is not always maximised by market offerings. The particular dynamics of the case determine the costs and benefits of each model.

In general then, Liberals assert that (in the economic sphere) the State should challenge monopoly; reduce the costs to citizens of gaining and exchanging information, and empower individual choice.

Scotland's own oligarchy

In *Who Owns Scotland*, Andy Wightman sets out in clear and shocking terms how much of Scotland is owned by how few people, and goes on to explain that this has been so for generations. Some of the great land owners are no longer individuals but corporate entities-effectively controlled in many cases by family placed trustees. Scotland: a place where a few hundred of "the great and the good" own territory occupied by over five million people.

Amending feudal land law and providing some community buy back rights with a claim on government resources was a Liberal step towards change by the coalition over the first two Scottish governments.

However, the governance of Scotland has been (and to a large extent still is) 'owned' by a few of the great and the good. For more than fifty years, the home grown 'great and good' were picked by the local monopoly of the Labour party. Since the creation of the Scottish Parliament some of that has changed. At a Scottish level this is as a result of a more proportionally elected chamber, and at a more local level, as a result of proportionality in local government forced on Labour by the Liberal Democrats.

However 'feudal' thinking about government in Scotland - that the great and the good shall rule (by appointment and therefore by patronage) has not fundamentally changed. The pool from which they are selected is now largely determined by the SNP. Whilst a change of personnel after so long is probably beneficial for its own sake, Liberal Democrats are keen to see change not only in the name on the box of privileged access but also in the structure of the governance of privilege. Liberal Democrats also have a central and continuing interest in seeking to break the monopoly of the power to nominate the oligarchy.

Once again, in general, Liberal Democrats assert that (in the political sphere) the State should challenge monopoly; reduce the costs to citizens of gaining and exchanging information, and empower individual choice. The reality is that few real world political transactions consist of two equally powerful and well informed individuals, freely exchanging well understood rights and duties to mutual advantage.

We implicitly recognise that organisational friction (the political equivalent of market failure) is universal but of varying degree when - despite the inherent biases in our system of legal appointment - many Liberal Democrats would argue against directly electing senior judges.

How is a balance to be struck between high levels of expertise and electoral accountability, between popular accountability and populism? Whilst simple distance between the electorate and administrative output should in principle be minimised, not all administrative forms of equal "length" are the same.

Selection, appointment or election?

The difference between an officer appointed to either the civil service or local government, and the head of one of the many structures that intermesh and control Scotland is that for the civil service or council position the criteria for selection and the process of appointment are regulated by rules applied to all posts of the same level by (in most cases) independent officers of the state who could (in theory) lose their job if they were unfair. The rules of selection are relatively testable.

It is of course true that (for example) in the case of Scottish Water, Creative Scotland, JESSICA, Scottish Universities, the choice of those running the institution is not absolutely arbitrary. After the civil service has provided some names and once the political patronage/ balance is taken into account, appointments could be justified by appeal to the experience and life history of those selected by the politicians. With a mixture of the usual suspects and patronage, a cadre of people who have "done this sort of thing before" is built up and drawn from. On this basis, many of the great and good might be appropriate people - were the "jobs" to be freely available.

There are however a large number of people who could (at least as justifiably) have been appointed, and then there are also the people appointed who are not really expected to do a job, but just be placed. At a Scotland wide level, on these sorts of Non-Departmental Public Bodies (NDPB), a very few people chose the heads, the board, and the chief executive. There is a problem in civil society when so many important organisations are 'overseen' by appointees.

In local government, the largest local authority in Scotland sits in a nexus of organisations. Glasgow has community planning partnerships that oversee significant community decision and spending, with people appointed from a whole range of bodies themselves detached from elected legitimacy. There are ALEOs (arms length organisations) that trade with representatives of the handpicked. There is a charity which now controls the museums and many of the halls and swimming pools that Glasgow city council once ran. It also defines library delivery, sport provision and music opportunity in Glasgow. It negotiates with the council about the services it provides for the cash the local authority will pay. It gets a tax advantage for not being a local government organisation.

One of the central problems with all this (for a Liberal Democrat) is that few Glaswegians will easily understand or in any way affect either its structure or its controlling membership. On its web site it is defined thus:

"Glasgow Life and the sub-brands mentioned above are the operating name(s) of Culture and Sport Glasgow (Trading) CIC ("CSG CIC"). CSG CIC is a community interest

company, registered in Scotland with company number SC313850"

On the CSG board (in August 2010) sit: six councillors plus: Rt Hon George Reid, Rt Hon The Lord Macfarlane of Bearsden KT, Sir Angus Grossart, Mel Young, and Dr Bridget McConnell.

On the CSG CIC board sit two of the same councillors and Dr Bridget McConnell plus: Dr Kenneth Christie, Lawyer, Senior Partner at McClure Naismith; Ed Crozier, Film/ Drama Producer & Rugby Referee; Seumas MacInnes, Restaurateur; Flora Martin, PR/ Marketing consultant.

Now all of these are fine people (some are titled people) but none were elected to these important jobs. Even the councillors were not **elected** as directors. It needs remembering that directors of boards or trustees of charities have different responsibilities and accountabilities in law to those required of elected councillors.

GL is perhaps the most diverse and visible of the non Glasgow council bodies that run Glasgow council functions. Another - CORDIA - runs the most vital care services in the city but (even with five councilors) it is not a part of the council.

A Liberal Democrat "solution"

A bonfire of the ALEOs / Quangos has been promised since time immemorial. Some come, some go, but it will take a self denying ordinance on the part of central government to forego an action point headline.

Accountability demands that we bring the job back to a general elected body. Sustained reduction at both local and national level can only be achieved by adherence to a general principle of "the non commutation of powers". By this I mean that people elected to bodies with wide powers and responsibilities should in general not be able to 'sub-contract' those powers to a body with non elected decision makers whose work cannot be directly controlled or overseen by the parent body. For those remaining, there needs to be a change in how they are run.

The majority of local government ALEOs exist to circumvent rules on tax, remuneration, or capital raising applied to the parent body. If Glasgow City Council could raise capital against well-audited commercial activity, and get charitable status for activities otherwise deemed 'charitable' by the relevant body, there would be no need to set up ALEOs.

Individuals asked to sit on boards look the same. This is true of the private sector and commercial companies. It should not be true of public bodies. There should be an aim to widen the 'pool' from which members are drawn, and to train this wider 'selectorate', to assist representation and wider civil society. One way to reduce this "monopolisation" effect might be to place a limit on multiple membership and serial membership of these sorts of body. The members of the board could also submit an individual report evaluating how they have personally contributed to the workings and aims of the board in the last year

Whatever structure the professional, largely unelected organisations take, all meetings should be open, all decisions challengeable, (possibly by structured appeal to the originating body, usually a council or government department). The secrecy of "commercial confidentiality" should not be applied to their internal affairs, and should be kept to a (legally challengeable) minimum when dealing with private individuals or private companies.

If there is a democratic deficit, why not directly elect people to the board even if some places are reserved for experts? This has of course been tried. Unfortunately direct election is not usually a viable solution. "Ordinary" people don't stand or vote for these sorts of body. As the Herald 10th June 2010 reported:

> *Only one in six people eligible to vote in Scotland's first health board elections returned their ballot papers, fuelling claims there is little appetite for the pilot project...Turnout in Dumfries and Galloway was 22.4%, out of an electorate of 118,361, while in Fife only 13.9% of 404,261 voters chose members of the boards...Health Secretary Nicola Sturgeon acknowledged turnout was lower than desired, but said the fact that 131 candidates stood for 22 positions across two trial areas showed people wanted to be involved in the NHS.*

"Punters" correctly suspect they would usually have no profound input on professionally structured boards. The time and trouble to become informed enough to contribute to one of these bodies tends to favour those who either worked in the controlled area for a living, for instance a doctor or teacher or transport executive, or have been on one of these bodies before. Lay board members, whilst nominally in charge, find it harder to make a real contribution rather than supinely agree to the professional advice. Local non specialists do care about their local GP surgery; and/ or their local bus service; and the swimming baths; and the primary school; - but they do not care (very much) about the whole NHS, or leisure policy or educational administration – certainly not enough to attempt to join *each* of the bodies that deal with *each* of these things.

Westminster appointed bodies need to cede power and resources to Holyrood and they in turn to local councils and they in turn to geographically small but general local bodies. One solution to the lack of general electoral interest in getting elected to arms length bodies would be to attempt to reformulate the basis of their existence (and operation) from topic specific (largely theoretical) control over a wide geographical area to general control of a local area. In a sense this reinvents very local councils. They could operate the way most people would want community councils to work. Elected "community planning" would be refreshing.

Empowerment requires people motivated to take part. In general people are more than keen to take "decisions that directly change my immediate surroundings" if that change happens in a relatively short time.

There are real problems of scale. The more local an organisation the more there is replication and a need for costly communication with other similar bodies sharing physical or functional boundaries. These are real problems, but co-ops of shared institutional resources are working right now (joint police/ fire boards, joint buying entities, joint pension fund arrangements, and community resource centres ...).

The great and the good will tell us that there is no need for all this fuss – that they have ever had the best interests of the rest of us at heart. Those who appoint and dismiss, will tell us all is under their control (ultimately the theoretical control of elected individuals, and therefore democracy reigns absolutely supreme). If we believe them - absolutely – we need do nothing.

If we think that there is a massive disenfranchisement at the core of appointed government, and further that a "bonfire of the Quango/Aleo/NDPBs" has failed, then a change in the mind-set of governance is needed. Let us not set up an appointed body to enforce the change.

Chapter 12

Lessons from the Arab Spring

Gillian Gloyer

The Arab Spring has reminded us, among other things, that democracy is not defined only by elections contested by political parties: revolutions, too, can be democratic. They can also, more unexpectedly, be liberal. What were the liberal characteristics of last year's uprisings in North Africa? How did they compare to earlier processes of régime change, in the Balkans and the former Soviet Union? How have the political élites in these countries recovered their control of the process? And does the Arab Spring have anything to teach Western political élites (us, for example) about how the people can express and implement their will?

The cutely named "colour revolutions" of the first decade of the millennium, in countries across the former Soviet Union from Belarus to Kyrgyzstan, were led by politicians, usually ones who had previously been involved in the governments which they were now trying to overthrow. The other key participants in those uprisings were non-party movements, funded and mentored by Western advisers, mostly from US-based organisations such as the National Democratic Institute for International Affairs (NDI, the author's employer from 1998 to 2002) and the International Republican Institute (IRI). These movements were inspired by (or, to be more accurate, copied from) Serbia and Montenegro's *Otpor*, which became pivotal in the overthrow of Slobodan Milošević. Otpor, and its avatars such as *Kmara* in Georgia and *Pora* in Ukraine, used cheap, instant text messaging to bring its supporters out on to the streets. Text messaging also played a fundamental role in the ability of civil society organisations to monitor elections before and after the "colour revolutions"; observers in each polling station communicated data on voter turn-out, suspicious activities and, finally, the outcome of the ballot count in that polling station, so that statisticians could calculate what the election result ought to be, before the Central Election Commission got its hands on the count data.

The use of new technologies was the only feature of the earlier uprisings which was shared by those of the Arab Spring. In Tunisia and Egypt, political parties had existed for years - some had been co-opted by the Ben Ali and Mubarak régimes, while others survived in real opposition, despite the imprisonment and exile of their leaders. Yet in both countries, the political parties were conspicuous by their absence from the demonstrations. These, like the uprisings which followed across the Maghreb and Middle East, were mobilisations of ordinary people. (Perhaps it is the absence of political parties from the uprisings which explains why there were so many women involved in them, even in more conservative countries such as Libya and Bahrain.)

The West's friendly relations with the dictatorships of the Maghreb meant that, unlike the Balkans or the former Soviet Union, the protesters there did not have access to foreign advice or funding. The European Union Delegation in Tunis, for example, was closely identified with the Ben Ali régime, and its advice is unlikely to have been welcome even if it had chosen to offer it to the protesters. There were no representatives on the ground of the US-based organisations, the German political foundations, or any other international non-governmental bodies. By the time they noticed what was going on, it was all over and Ben Ali had fled into exile.

Technology had advanced since the "colour revolutions". Rather than text messages, the participants in the Arab Spring used Twitter and Facebook to communicate with each other, and YouTube to transmit images of their protests to the rest of the world. This latter feature was greatly enhanced by the fact that, although spoken Arabic differs widely from one region to another, the written language is identical throughout the Arab world. The uprising in Syria began when some young people wrote on a wall the words which they had seen in YouTube pictures from Tunisia and Egypt: "The people want the government to go".

Collaboratively led, rather than vertically hierarchical; visibly supported by people of all ages and both sexes, rather than dominated by middle-aged men; free from outside influence, whether well-meaning or malign - how on earth were the political élites to rescue themselves from this scary, unfamiliar environment? The answer, of course, is through elections.

Competition between internally accountable political parties, within an equitable and pluralist framework, is undoubtedly a more efficient mechanism for selecting the people's representatives than a horizontally structured group of people camping in a public square. But what happens where political parties like this, and a framework like this, have never existed? In Tunisia, the first post-revolution elections, to a temporary Constituent Assembly (or constitutional convention), were contested by almost 1,500 lists of candidates across the 27 constituencies into which the country was divided (voters in one constituency, in Greater Tunis, had 95 candidate lists to choose from!). Most of these lists were presented by political parties: some long-established, whether or not they had been legal under the old régime; others, newly formed splinter groups from older parties or thinly disguised reincarnations of the former party of government; and some, little more than one man (invariably) and his dog. Over a third of the lists, though, were made up of 'independents', in many cases genuinely independent businesspeople or professionals who had no political ambitions but felt they had something to contribute to the drafting of their country's new constitution. One might have thought - and many of these independent candidates obviously did think - that voters would favour the same sort of people who had driven Ben Ali from power, rather than the political parties which had sat on the sidelines. But in the end, they behaved like voters in any established democracy, and mostly supported proper parties which they knew something about. None of the genuinely independent candidates was elected. However, there is considerable diversity of opinion within the Constituent Assembly, and the chances seem good that the constitution which emerges at the end of the drafting process will reflect that diversity.

In Egypt, too, a few political parties had managed to survive the years of dictatorship. As in Tunisia, the party which has won the most votes is a long-standing opposition force (the Muslim Brotherhood) which advocates respect for Muslim values rather than hard-line secularism or Salafism. Here, though, the old régime has proved more adept than in Tunisia at clinging to power. The liberal aspirations of the Egyptian revolution may be sidelined as the regional bosses of the Mubarak era forge alliances with the Muslim Brotherhood and with the army.

Although the post-revolutionary elections have gone well in Tunisia and Egypt, they could quite easily end up making matters worse in other countries in the region. Elections can prove fatal to fledgling democracies. One danger is that they exacerbate tribal or religious divisions - Iraq and Afghanistan are textbook examples of this. In Côte d'Ivoire, when presidential elections finally took place in 2010, they very nearly led to the breakdown of the fragile peace agreement and to the recrudescence of civil war. The alternative risk is that elections do nothing but entrench existing power structures. Examples of this are Kyrgyzstan and Georgia, where politicians who had previously been associated with the ruling party overthrew it, but then went on to replicate its corruption and arrogation of power. It is not difficult to imagine the former outcome in Libya and, if the uprising in Syria is eventually successful, the latter outcome there.

What might political élites like ours learn from the Arab revolutions, or from their predecessors elsewhere? A cynical one might be that we have no need to worry. Activists can camp in St Andrew's Square for as long as they like but, come the next election, the voters will stick with the political parties they know. The flaw in this strategy is that it will widen still further the gulf between the political class and the people whom it is supposed to represent. Chile's students spent almost the whole of the 2011 academic year on strike, campaigning for the abolition of tuition fees and other reforms to the education system, yet they have had no discernible impact on the discourse within either of the country's main political alliances. The parliamentary opposition has been unable to engage convincingly with the students, while the government apparently thinks it can outlast them - the same approach as politicians in the UK and US seem to have towards the Occupy movements. In established democracies like these, the inability of politicians to respond to popular protest is unlikely to lead to revolution or civil war, as it has done in the Arab world, but it is hardly satisfactory if protestors and politicians operate in parallel universes.

Perhaps we are too close to the political process to see its flaws in the way that ordinary, disaffected people do. Our parties offer the electorate a choice between options which are presented as being almost identical (it doesn't help that *we* know that they are not). Our media are supine, self-censoring out any diversity of viewpoint. Our (Scottish) government anaesthetises us with populist slogans and low-cost bribes. It all sounds depressingly like Tunisia before its revolution - all that's missing are political prisoners. No wonder most people see no connection between themselves and the political establishment.

Social networking has changed the nature of political communication. In Iceland, the draft articles of the new constitution are being posted on Facebook and Twitter, where citizens can comment directly on them. Of course, Iceland's population is smaller than that of Edinburgh, but it is an interesting initiative on which we might be able to build. We need to become better at listening to what people are saying on-line, in the same way as we used to try to listen to people 'off-line' in the days of community politics. Then we need to learn, or remember, how to translate their concerns into political proposals which might somehow be achievable. Despite what we are constantly told by opinion pollsters, ordinary people *are* interested in social justice and civil liberties. This is what the Tunisians and Egyptians who peacefully overthrew their governments wanted; it is what the Occupy movement wants, basically. The challenge for us is to find language which expresses our principles in a way which is intelligible outside the corridors of power, and to communicate it in a way which reaches the people who currently believe that we and they have nothing to say to each other.

Chapter 13

The Way Forward

Nigel Lindsay and Robert Brown

The authors represented in this book of essays cover many subjects, but some common themes and trends emerge again and again.

- Helplessness – I can't change things

- Resignation – nothing I do will stop them

- The arrogance of power - the power of the rich and well-connected opposed to the impotence of the rest

- Lack of Choice – what are the choices for the disadvantaged?

- Powerlessness – and the need for social mechanisms that can compensate for it.

These are dangerous trends, if we have identified them correctly. They speak first of the emergence of an underclass, as Robert Brown has identified elsewhere in this volume, an underclass robbed of money, power, and morale by political trends and social decay that have yet to be challenged effectively. Their second message is of a widespread conviction among those who have been belittled in this way, that there is no further point in political engagement or participation in debate. Even winning the debate does not seem to alter the Zeitgeist, and has no effect on the distribution of power and resources in the country where we live.

The second of these is the one capable of causing most lasting damage. It may seem futile to rail against the Leviathan of power and money represented so clearly in the recent financial crisis, but to surrender in cynicism will hand lasting victory to those who seek to arrogate the nation's resources to themselves. To assert the truth of that is not to suggest it is easy to keep on campaigning for a more just society. After all, the evidence shows that such campaigns have often not led to real change. And it is unreasonable to expect people to struggle on their own - they need a voice in the political system.

That voice should come from the political parties traditionally opposed to the extension of privilege, but it is not immediately clear how this can be the case. The Labour Party has been wholly sucked into the world of bankers and stock markets since the days of Blair and it cannot speak with conviction for those who have been harmed by these interests. A more reliable voice should be that of the Liberal Democrats, but there are obvious limitations on our power within the Coalition to fulfil that function.

Coalition Government is a difficult place for both partners – but particularly the junior partner. Liberal

Democrat Ministers have injected a significant level of greater fairness into the Government's approach and are thankfully becoming more skilled at promoting the distinct Liberal Democrat contribution in government - and the Party has won worthy battles on specific Government policy areas. But it is questionable whether we are yet exerting enough influence in government to reverse the imbalances of power and wealth identified in this volume. Raising the tax free bar to £10,000 will undoubtedly help many low and middle income families, but, if the overall trend, as Elspeth Attwooll notes, is towards still further widening of the gap between rich and poor, it is clear that significant additional measures are required.

In a similar way, the focus now being given by Nick Clegg, Vince Cable and others to top people's pay and the over-concentration of power is welcome but must result in concrete action which will lead to the wealthiest and most powerful people in the UK making a full fair contribution to the national pot. Choice is important but it must be based on a recognition of how little choice the poorest people have, and how low on their priorities choice is. As John Aldridge points out, for many people, what matters is the effectiveness of the service they achieve rather than choice of provider.

It is implicit in this volume that it is now time for Liberal Democrats to articulate the concerns of those who want to challenge the trends listed above. It is urgent for us to do so for two main reasons. The first of these is that these matters are corroding our society, corrupting the beneficiaries and demoralizing the others. The second is that if there is no major political party prepared to articulate and act on the concerns of the majority, then faith in democracy will quickly ebb away and decision-making will fall more and more into the hands of spin-doctors and professional lobbyists. That in turn would make the political climate easier for extremists and demagogues and wholly inimical to Liberalism.

Liberal Democrats have always believed that the way to redistribute resources is first to redistribute power. If power is shared fairly, a fairer distribution of wealth is likely to follow. We believe this argument resonates with the public and that, just as much as the priority given to the deficit, the Party should again seek to become a voice for empowering communities, putting the general interest much more at the heart of the ethos and practice of companies, and standing on the side of those whose life chances are compromised by the actions of the greedy and the powerful and the social trends they produce.. The Coalition is doing things that the Conservatives by themselves would not have done, and this should continue to be an important part of our role. Ultimately we are the conscience of the Coalition.

This is not to say that reducing the deficit is unimportant. Liberals have always believed in sound finance and will continue to do so. But it is time for a new and empirical approach in which Liberal Democrats start not from the demands of the financial markets but from the needs of the people and how these can best be met by Liberal methods.

We believe that the Party needs to seek a new direction, one in which it is committed to economic decisions being controlled by political considerations rather than vice versa, and where the needs of the powerless are put before those of oligarchs and directors of supranational companies. It would be futile to deny that taking this direction will necessitate rebuilding the trust of the voters, which has been unfortunately compromised. But if that is done in good conscience, and people once again start to listen to what we say, we shall find before long that we speak for a majority of the electorate.

Demonstrating true public support will enhance our authority as junior coalition partners. It will give us real power to influence political change, both within and outside government. Nick Clegg says, rightly, that we cannot get everything we want in government because we did not win the election (though neither, it must be added, did David Cameron). We shall be able to get a great deal more if we can show we can carry the people with us – and indeed that we can mobilise an increasing public support in elections.

A first step should be to make an honest assessment of what has been achieved by Liberal Democrats within the Coalition's first two years. This should examine performance against the Coalition Agreement, put achievements in perspective, and look also at legislation passed that was not foreseen in the Agreement (such as the proposed NHS reforms in England). To do this is simply good management. Any worthwhile and properly-managed enterprise will, at regular intervals, monitor performance and assess achievements against targets. Our participation in the coalition deserves no less.

Such a process will reveal where we have been successful, and also where there is scope for us to achieve more. It will be an important pointer to how Liberal Democrat MPs and Ministers can work best for the electorate and for the principles of the Party they represent, and should be done primarily by rank-and-file members of the Party.

While this process is in train, there should be a renewal of debate within the Party on the specific policies we need for the future. What actions do we need to pursue to achieve our aims of redistributing power, ending the helplessness so many people feel, and building a new and more just society? What should we be asking Ministers to do, and what can we do ourselves?

The authors and editors of *The Little Yellow Book* have not laid out a programme of new, specific policies – that is properly work for all Party members. What we hope we have done is to set out an analysis of the present hindrances to building a Liberal society, and to suggest directions of travel which will lead us all to the necessary policy specifics. The ideas within the *Book* are not prescriptive, but intend to set light to a wide-ranging debate within and outside the Party, involving all Party members, and people with vision who are sympathetic to the ideals of Liberalism but not yet in the Party.

Liberalism has a tremendous heritage of ideas and values on which to draw, supplemented since May 2010 by the harsh experiences and lessons of government. Now, more than ever before, Liberal ideas are needed in the face of unprecedented challenges. Let that debate commence now.